The Elements of Visual Analysis

Marguerite Helmers

University of Wisconsin, Oshkosh

PEARSON
Longman

New York   San Francisco   Boston
London   Toronto   Sydney   Tokyo   Singapore   Madrid
Mexico City   Munich   Paris   Cape Town   Hong Kong   Montreal

Senior Acquisitions Editor: Lynn M. Huddon
Executive Marketing Manager: Megan Galvin-Fak
Production Manager: Donna DeBenedictis
Project Coordination, Text Design, and Electronic Page Makeup:
    Elm Street Publishing Services, Inc.
Cover Designer/Manager: Wendy Ann Fredericks
Manufacturing Manager: Mary Fischer
Printer and Binder: R.R. Donnelley & Sons Company/Harrisonburg
Cover Printer: The Lehigh Press, Inc.

Library of Congress Cataloging-in-Publication Data

Helmers, Marguerite H., 1961–
    The elements of visual analysis / Marguerite Helmers.—1st ed.
        p. cm.
    ISBN 0-321-16525-X (alk. paper)
    1. Visual communication.   2. Rhetoric.   I. Title.

P93.5.H456 2006
302.23—dc22   2005030466

Please visit us at www.ablongman.com

ISBN 0-321-16525-X

1 2 3 4 5 6 7 8 9 10—DOH—08 07 06 05

Contents

iii

Contents

Preface for Instructors

It would be difficult to deny the prevalence and importance of visual media in today's society. The students entering our classrooms today have grown up with hundreds of channels of television, and the World Wide Web is no longer a novelty but part of their everyday lives. When we consider the nonelectronic sources of visuals such as billboards, print advertisements, and colorful packaging design have taken such an important place in our consumer culture, then we have to conclude that most of the information that our students are exposed to is in a visual form.

Because outside the classroom our students engage relatively rarely with *verbal* text, we might be tempted to think that their lives are devoid of information or of expression. However, quite the opposite is true. Our students may have been exposed to more "texts" in the form of images than any other generation in history, and many of these image texts are dense with cultural information. One might argue that many image texts are designed mostly for entertainment or to sell something rather than to offer information or increase understanding of complex issues; nevertheless, our students are exposed to a broad range of communicative media daily. What our educational system has failed to take seriously and to respond to is the fact that so much of this information is packaged in visual forms.

Arguably, the primary purpose of study in literature, language, and rhetoric is to teach students to respond to the messages that they will encounter throughout their lives. Given this objective, and given that so many of the messages that our students encounter are and will continue to be visual in nature, it no longer seems viable for teachers in departments of English and communication to continue to ignore the visual. Many books on the college market address visual thinking, making it possible to offer an entire course on imagery.

The ubiquity of visuals is not the only reason why educators should devote more attention to their analysis. Barbara Stafford argues for the unique expressive and epistemic power of images, pointing out that they can be used to discover and to express "that which could not otherwise be known." In other words, images can serve to express distinct valuable concepts that simply cannot be put into words, and these non-verbal concepts or feelings are valuable in their own right. Advertisers and politicians understand and take advantage of the unique powers of images, but as long as we neglect them in our classes, our students cannot take advantage of these powers or even effectively respond to visual messages.

The boundary separating text from image has always been little more than a convenient way to keep one academic division from encroaching too liberally on the specialty of another. As new computer technologies become more sophisticated and more dominant, the separation of visual thought from verbal invention, drafting, revision, and publication is almost impossible, as the words on the electronic page (the computer screen) take a visual form: they are embedded in a Graphical User Interface (GUI) of toolbars, scroll bars, and WYSIWYG formatting. For a long time, embedding any kind of visual into one's writing was possible only for professional writers; it often involved several people working separately and was a complex and expensive process. Today, however, anyone who writes on a computer can embed images into his or her text. A standard word processing package contains numerous options for incorporating visual elements, and the World Wide Web, which is quickly becoming the standard mode of transmission for many types of texts, relies largely on visual elements for its impact and its attraction. Visual elements are more than just decoration; they are integral structural ideas.

Traditional high school and college textbooks, especially those in English and the humanities, incorporate visual material. Many times, this information is positioned to illustrate an historical concept—some person, place, or thing that the modern consciousness cannot call to mind.

The Elements of Visual Analysis is intended as a supplement of the primary readings of a college literature or writing course. It can also be used in other courses in the humanities. While it is not a book on writing instruction, new media development, or graphic design (these subjects are admirably addressed by full-course texts), it does provide instructors and students with ideas for writing and presenting projects based on the critical subject matter presented in the chapters. Instructors who are interested in adding a visual culture component to an existing writing, literature, or speech course will find the book useful. *The Elements of Visual Analysis* covers historical periods and styles from the nineteenth century to the present; addressing issues such as the representation of landscapes and people, the critical concepts and topics of the book can be used to extend backward in time to other eras and media.

In *The Elements of Visual Analysis*, students are invited to explore beyond the printed page, to visit art museums and galleries and historic and contemporary sites that employ strong visual elements to create a sense of place and time. Whether you use one chapter or one assignment, or explore the contents of the entire book, *The Elements of Visual Analysis* should enable your students to study a variety of image texts and begin their own independent analyses of visual culture.

I would like to thank all those who reviewed and provided feedback on drafts of the manuscript. Lisa Snow, who created the glossary, deserves thanks for her good ideas and tolerance. Eric Arima, Angel Chavez, Angela Gelsomino, and Jonathan Lyzun at Elm Street Publishing were an incredible help in seeing the project through the production process. Finally, thanks to Bill, Emily, and Caitlin, whose willingness to put up with their own scribbling woman should never go unacknowledged.

MARGUERITE HELMERS

Preface for Students

Look around. You are surrounded by pictures, images, and visual displays: advertisements, billboards, television commercials, the evening news. You have probably taken photographs at events like family vacations, graduations, holidays, or sports competitions. You may play with photographs on an electronic editor. Your textbooks—from history, to Western civilization, to English—include illustrations. Sometimes these are portraits of the authors, sometimes they are complementary illustrations from the time period that is being studied.

Because visual information is so ubiquitous, many teachers are asking students to conduct visual analyses. *The Elements of Visual Analysis* is intended to provide background on critical terms and approaches for students enrolled in courses that study the intersection of language, communication, and media. While the use of images in college classrooms is not new, increasingly students are asked to investigate topics such as race and gender through imagery. Images are used conceptually to open up discussion of topics such as **representation** and **ideology**. Many images found in courses in literature, communication, and humanities are traditional photographs, cartoons, and paintings. What if you were to consider these as dynamic, **performative** visual materials? In other words, how would your view of the illustrations change if you studied them as instruments used to affect, if not persuade, the audience of viewers?

How do you begin? How can you write an insightful essay without just telling what you see or narrating the story of the image? This book is designed to give you a starting point for conducting analyses of a variety of visual material. What does *The Elements of Visual Analysis* offer you?

- Sample essays demonstrating how professional writers create analyses of visual culture
- Defined critical terms to build vocabulary on visual subjects

- Suggested visual subjects to write about, including photography, landscape, and fine art
- A bibliography of works for further research

Each chapter features assignment ideas that draw on chapter concepts and examples:

- **Re-Vision** questions and assignments invite you to create your own analyses of key images in each chapter.
- **In Focus: Image and Analysis** directs you to apply the concepts and questions introduced in each chapter to image texts of your own choosing. The In Focus sections can be used to initiate an independent project.
- **On Display** offers a new image, related to the chapter topic, as a writing or discussion prompt.

A brief handbook such as this can provide only a few examples for you to begin your investigations. The examples of visual information provided in this book are of people and places. Within each chapter, particular terms are brought to the fore that will enable a critical analysis of the subject. The images used here range from family snapshots to famous paintings and photographs. Some are contemporary; some are historical. Chapter One introduces you to the basic concepts of visual culture studies. Chapter Two focuses on the elements of design such as color, line, and texture. Chapter Three investigates place. Chapter Four examines positive and negative representations of people. Seek out further examples and applications of the ideas and concepts introduced in each chapter. There is literally a world of visual ideas in front of you.

Remember that, whenever possible, take yourself to places where you can see original images. Try to move away from reproductions in books and on the Internet to broaden your experiences with the different types of media that are used to create visual imagery, from sculpture to painting to interior design.

M. H.

1

Visual Culture
The World of Images and Texts

What Are You Looking At?

When you walk down the street, how many images do you see? You probably will notice signs for businesses, such as the golden arches of McDonald's. You might see a billboard advertising a restaurant or a sightseeing destination. Do you recognize any logos for name-brand objects? Do the people you pass on the street wear shirts, caps, jackets, or shoes that display images or icons like the Nike swoosh? Stop at the corner and look at the walk sign, another icon. The stoplights above it use color to tell drivers how to handle their cars: stop, go, use caution.

All of these uses of fashion, signs, images, and icons are a part of American **visual culture**—and they are subjects for written analysis. As media pundits and educators tell us, for better or for worse contemporary society is dominated by images. Efforts to provide the American public with the tools of **visual literacy** are increasingly placed at the forefront of educational efforts.

Images are created to express an idea or emotion. Images are used to imagine alternatives, to create new ways of looking at something. Images record parts of the world that are inaccessible to the majority of the public, document major events, or examine emotions that are at the

1

extreme ends of pain or pleasure. Images communicate: they motivate, persuade, or warn.

When educators and media commentators argue that ours is a visual culture, they are indicating that images are the primary mode of communication and expression in contemporary society, replacing verbal composition and expression. The term **visual culture** is of recent origin and derives from work in art history, sociology, and cultural studies. The three primary modes of communication in contemporary society are the written word, the spoken word, and the use of images. Visual culture studies emphasize that images convey meanings, perhaps even more so than the written word. Those interested in studying the visual aspects of contemporary culture include in their perspective fashion, photography, dance, opera, musical theater, electronic images, medical illustrations, advertising, billboards, graphic design, museum displays, film, television, architecture, public sculpture, and industrial design. The approaches used to study images are primarily political, questioning who has the money and access to materials to produce and distribute images and how social and gendered groups (such as men, women, African Americans, and Native Americans) have been depicted in the media that are publicly available.

A third term, **visual rhetoric**, refers to the way that images persuade viewers to adopt attitudes or perform certain actions. **Propaganda** is one type of persuasive visual image that is designed to affect how viewers see the world—or people—around them. American war posters from World War I and World War II frequently featured broad caricatures of Germans and Japanese. These cartoon-like drawings were designed to make an "enemy" look as hideous, demonic, and nonhuman as possible in order to allow for more patriotic feeling for the Allies. Propagandistic caricature served as shorthand for national expression.

Advertisers also use images to persuade consumers to purchase particular products or services or to undertake certain actions, such as joining the Army. This use of images to persuade is called a "rhetorical use" of the image. However, many images affect viewers in particular emotional or intellectual ways and are not advertisements or instances of propaganda. Part of what you will think about in this book is how visual culture persuades us. Visual cultural studies are not limited to **two-dimensional** print objects such as cosmetic advertisements or children's book illustrations. Even **three-dimensional** objects such as cars are constructed to persuade us to purchase them. For example, cars have a particular color scheme that is gender-biased. While there is nothing intrinsically "unmasculine" about the color pink, messages in our culture condition young men to avoid that color choice. (Even the idea that there is something essentially "male" or "female" is constructed through messages in our society.) When purchasing a car from the dealer's lot, a petal pink Dodge Ram 4 × 4 pickup would not be a persuasive color option for a young man. Again, there is nothing essentially "feminine" about pink. That color has been repeatedly used in our culture to denote "femininity," therefore we have been persuaded by this association. Most automobiles are offered in colors that are assumed to be gender-neutral, such as black, red, white, and blue. These sell to the widest audience because they are generally free of culturally coded associations.

At a very broad level, then, we can say that images are used to express attitudes toward subjects in the world. Regardless of whether someone owns a television or picks up a copy of *People* magazine at the grocery store, no one is entirely free of images in our culture or their persuasive qualities. Visual culture studies help us to realize that we never simply look. We are constantly engaged in a process of looking and forming an opinion about what we see. We make judgments of taste when we like or dislike the "look" of something. We can act out of cultural bias or prejudice when we refuse to "look beyond the surface." We can react emotionally—with tears or laughter—when we see something that moves us.

Why do these reactions occur? Are there basic ways that people react to images? What are some of the common elements of visual display that persuade viewers—consciously or unconsciously—to react in particular ways? As you read this book and see the images around you, ask yourself these questions. By asking "Why?" you will begin to solve

> **Discuss**
>
> Visit two websites and compare their color schemes and design schemes. Can you tell whether they are designed with a female audience or a male audience in mind? Some sites to consider are the National Football League (**www.nfl.com**) and Oprah! (**www.oprah.com**).

problems, respond reflectively and creatively to the myriad of images in our society, and construct a meaning from the world around you.

Experimenting with Image, Word, and Sound

When you were young, you probably drew pictures in school. Now, you most likely take photographs to commemorate events in your life, such as graduations and birthdays. All of those images collected in your home and all of the visual experiences you have had in your life can become the subjects for analysis. Here are some activities to get you started thinking visually. Use these ideas for journaling, group projects, or formal essays.

- Listen to a popular song or a folk song. Find an image that seems to go with that song. Ask yourself why the image expresses the emotional content of the song. Is it possible that a different image would yield a different interpretation of the same song? When writing about this, you will be working with **multimodal** forms of expression, combining sound and image to create meaning.

- Have someone take a photograph of you. Using this portrait as the basis for a metaphor, journal on the prompt, "I am like. . . ." Describe the ways that the photo portrait conveys your beliefs and attitudes.

- Create a collage of images drawn from magazines or newspapers that reflects you and your life history and interests. Select four or five key moments in your life to illustrate. This is often referred to as a "life graph." Compose a prose statement that goes with the piece. Present the image and narrative to the class.

- Bring an object to class that is meaningful to you. Have a partner look at it objectively and describe its shape, size, color, and use as if the object were being catalogued for a museum. Then, describe what the object means to you. Compare the two responses to the object. What does each prose description capture? What is missing from either description? What are the tangible elements of the object that cannot be captured by words?

Text and Image

Two-dimensional images in print, such as those in magazines and newspapers, are sometimes seen as purely decorative or as **illustrations** for text. In this conception, the image cannot be separated from the text. It depends on written language to make it intelligible, in other words, to make it "make sense."

Cartoons are familiar formats that regularly use images and text to convey ideas. We are familiar with this form from childhood, when the daily "funny papers" are passed to us from the newspaper. Political cartooning has a long and distinguished history extending back several hundred years to seventeenth-century Europe. Comics use a sophisticated shorthand of visual elements to convey motion and the relationship between characters, such as viewing angle, close-ups, and lines. Traditional elements in the comics help us to read and understand them: "thought balloons" hold speech, lines drawn around figures indicate motion such as running or shaking, and bodies of humans and animals stretch disproportionately to emphasize movement. We may not question, though, which is the most dominant aspect of the cartoon: is it the text or the image? Is a comic or a cartoon possible without the text?

> **Freewrite**
>
> Create a double-entry journal by drawing a line down the center of your page.
>
> In the left-hand column, list as many types of images as you can see around you or think of. In the right-hand column, consider what purpose these images may have (such as providing information or persuading consumers).

For example, without text, this cartoon by California artist Bud Pisarek could be a picture of two cute angels gazing down upon Earth. Perhaps it appeared in a religious publication. The angel on the right looks rather wistful. Perhaps the angel on the right is a recent addition to the heavenly host and is thoughtfully considering what he (or she) has left behind in the material world below. The angel on the left appears to be speaking to him. Perhaps he is consoling the angel, reminding him of the riches of the eternal world to which he now belongs. What can you say about these angels?

"Above All," 17 July 2003
© Bud Pisarek

Here is the cartoon again, this time with the text that Pisarek added to their conversation.

"Above All," 17 July 2003
© Bud Pisarek

With the words added to the image, the angel on the right suddenly appears "worldly wise" and a bit of a rebel, ignoring holy messages and timeless religious thought to study spurious "messages" from UFOs. Even more extreme, he defies conventional religious traditions to study "crop circles," messages supposedly cut into cornfields by alien visitors from outer space. Is he dissatisfied by Eternity?

In rhetorical studies, the argument that images are dependent on text to "mean" something has been used to say that pictures are not persuasive. Yet, we recognize that our vision persuades us daily: an attractive display of patio furniture and patioware in Wal-Mart helps us purchase and decorate; an actress in flip-flops on the cover of *People* magazine helps to convince us that these beach shoes are acceptable for daily wear; a swimsuit model on the cover of *Sports Illustrated* convinces us to buy the magazine.

In the case of the cartoon "Above All," the image alone convinces us of many things that we accept immediately, based on our previous encounters with images of angels and political cartooning. While Pisarek's cartoon ran in the Auburn *Journal* in the midsize American city of Auburn, California, during the last decade, that contextual information isn't necessary to recognize that this one-frame image is from a **genre** of editorial cartooning that appears in newspapers and magazines such as the *New York Times*, the *Wall Street Journal*, and the *New Yorker*. We can also recognize that the cartoon is a humorous drawing that reflects current events and is not meant through its illustration to represent reality accurately.

For example, based on the range of cartoons in national publications, we are accustomed to seeing speaking dogs, cats, and birds. Angels, therefore, are just another example of the "speaking subject" and are an appropriate subject for political cartoons. Pisarek relies on the positive association that many viewers have with angels; the reading public finds them to be trustworthy and sympathetic. Angel images appear in many popular secular forms. The chubby duo of angels painted by Renaissance painter Raphael adorns checks, umbrellas, coffee mugs, tote bags, switch plates, and key chains.

Pisarek's angels are drawn as sexless and somewhat amorphous beings, unlike the more fully realized humanlike and almost lifelike

Discuss

Speaking animals are favorites of cartoonists and advertisers. Find examples of this and share them with your classmates. Does the message change if the words are removed? Why are animals popular subjects for cartoonists?

angels of Renaissance art, yet they draw on the tradition of cartoon art, which frequently exaggerates bodily features such as the heads and facial features of political features. Also, like most imagery of heavenly beings, these angels are fitted with halos, a traditional artistic **convention** that identifies them as sanctified. Reading the image, we accept that these angels have small wings that could not possibly bear the weight of their bodies (yet somehow these wings must allow the angels to fly, since that is what angels do). Like the cherubim of the Renaissance, these angels also enjoy resting on clouds. The angels of "Above All" also take an interest in the material world below, which leads us to conclude (also from the drawing) that angels have a social life and conversations among themselves.

Frequently, Pisarek's cartoon angels comment on the presidency, on national security, on war, and on foibles of consumer society. None of these textual thoughts are necessary, though, to understand "Above All"'s subject, genre, and major features. Thus, even in a form that we take for granted, the dependency of the image on the word is not a given. We understand the cartoon because of visual cartoon language, elements of visual expression that transfer from one image context to another. Chapter Four of this book expands the idea of how visual cues characterize people, in both positive and negative ways.

Many writers, from journalists to academics, consider how images shape perceptions and reflect societal concerns. Because they are analyzing the structure of images and deriving meaning from them, their published work echoes the type of analysis you are often asked to do in your classes. We recognize that the meanings we find in images extend beyond those that the imagemakers intended. We share cultural knowledge and memories with other viewers that make images intelligible. We also bring a store of personal experience to the viewing situation that affects how we emotionally respond to any image. Furthermore, our reactions can change over time so that an image to which we were once emotionally attached has very little meaning in later years.

There is no one method or best practice for analyzing images. Art historians, media critics, and reviewers for newspapers and magazines all focus on different aspects of images when they compose their written pieces. In addition, each two-dimensional image and three-dimensional object requires its own method of analysis.

For example, Robert Scholes, a former professor of literature at Brown University in Rhode Island, established a useful method for reading images in his book *Protocols of Reading* (1983). Referring to his analytic scheme of a photograph by American photojournalist W. Eugene Smith as a "protocol"—a description of the practice of making meaning—Scholes offers readers an accessible approach to understanding the problems of reading various types of "texts."

While his subject, a photograph entitled *Tomoko Uemura in Her Bath* (Minamata, Japan 1972), is no longer available for publication, Scholes's practice of looking and making meaning is a model for conducting visual analyses. *Tomoko Uemura in Her Bath* is a black-and-white photograph of a woman bathing her severely disfigured daughter in a large, square wooden bath. The woman gazes lovingly at the girl, who appears to be about fourteen or fifteen years old. The image was published in *Life* magazine in 1972, part of an effort to raise awareness of the effects of industrial pollution in Japan. Scholes embarks on a process of reading the image that breaks down into five steps, with rereading being a key process in each:

> **Key Point**
>
> Always reread images. A second look can tell you more than the first glance!

1. First reactions: recognize emotional impact
2. First rereading: examine formal elements
3. Second rereading: identify publication context and original audience
4. Third rereading: investigate who took the image, why the image was made, and the creator's decisions about subject matter
5. Fourth rereading: reconsider the emotional reaction

First Reactions: Emotion

Scholes asserts that we cannot fully appreciate how the image works upon us until we reread it. "First reactions" must become more aware; it is essential to move beyond them to achieve a level of understanding of the image. Scholes's first reaction to Smith's *Tomoko* is emotional; he finds the image disturbing because he cannot translate the form of Tomoko to any human form with which he is familiar.

First Rereading: Formal Elements

Scholes's initial level of rereading focuses on the structural elements of the image, what he calls the inner text. We can call these the **formal**

elements of the image because they relate to the form, or design and arrangement, of the entire composition. These **literal elements** are the "humanoid figure" that he has struggled to decode as human, an older woman, and bathtub. He notes that we use a "mental template"—our previous experience with and knowledge of forms—to understand the elements of the image (just as we did when understanding Pisarek's angels from the halos, wings, and clouds).

Second Level of Rereading: Publication

Scholes considers the **cultural context** in which the image was initially published (*Life* magazine, 1972) and the political consequences of the publication of the image (awareness of the effects of industrial pollution). This level of reading engages the image as a persuasive document, one that can make a difference in the lives of many people.

Third Level of Rereading: Process of Creation

Scholes moves from a brief discussion of the publication of the image in *Life* to quote Smith's description of why he took the image. Citing an interview with Smith, Scholes allows us a glimpse of the artist's technique. Readers learn that Smith lived with the subjects of his photographic research and came to know them as friends. After a time in the fishing village, he knew what type of image he wanted to take. The reader is then asked to question whether the fact that Smith didn't just "find" this image by chance changes its meaning in any way.

> **Key Point**
>
> Robert Scholes's Five-Point Sequence of Analysis
>
> 1. Emotional reaction
> 2. Formal elements
> 3. Publication history
> 4. Process of creation
> 5. Reconsidering emotional reaction

Fourth Level of Rereading: Rereading Emotion

Scholes argues that it is important, but not sufficient, to leave the analysis at the historical and political level. He comes full circle to the emotional reaction the viewer has to the image, validating the emotional, initial response as a basis for analysis. However, he turns the critical eye to address the emotion, finding it insufficient for a complete or complex analysis. In fact, through rereading, his initial ambivalence about this image of Tomoko Uemura—in which he found neither beauty nor understanding—turns to a deep appreciation for the image and affection for its subjects.

Writer at Work

In the following excerpt from a book chapter titled "Photographs, Writing, and Critical Thinking," authors Carol Hovanec and David Freund consider several viewing techniques similar to Robert Scholes's. Their subject is American photographer Jacob Riis's Ready for Sabbath Eve in a Coal Cellar, A Cobbler on Ludlow Street, *originally published in the 1890s. They are interested in the* historical background *of the image's production; they describe their emotional reaction to the image; and they support their discussion of the image with an itemization of the* **formal elements** *of the photograph.*

> **Key Point**
>
> Hovanec and Freund's Four-Point Sequence of Analysis
>
> 1. Publication history
> 2. Emotional reaction
> 3. Formal elements
> 4. Consider alternative meanings

Photographs, Writing, and Critical Thinking

Carol P. Hovanec and David Freund
Ramapo College of New Jersey

In Jacob Riis's famous 1890s work *How the Other Half Lives*, the photographs and text were planned to raise the consciousness of middle- and upper-class New Yorkers who were ignorant of or indifferent to conditions in the tenements of the Lower East

Hovanec, Carol P. and David Freund. "Photographs, Writing, and Critical Thinking." *Images in Language, Media, and Mind.* Ed. Roy F. Fox. Copyright © 1994 by the National Council of Teachers of English.

Side. Riis intended to shock these readers with indisputable statistics, brutal anecdotes, and graphic illustrations. Though the immigrants themselves did not read of babies suffocating or men living in coal bins, their descendants see and study this inhumanity in our classes today. Riis was striving to sensitize the wealthier people of his time, who were ignorant of the slum-dwellers' squalor, or who were indifferent because their visual experience of "the other half" included only the romanticized images that were often used to portray them.

In the carefully titled photograph *Ready for Sabbath Eve in a Coal Cellar, A Cobbler on Ludlow Street,* Riis shocks us with the cobbler's degrading living conditions. The power and economy of the details that communicate this degradation, as well as a subtler, contrasting idea, are the photograph's main strengths. First we are struck by the grime of the place and the incongruity of household furnishings in such a setting. Our attention is quickly drawn to the man because his bright face emerges vividly from the darker background and because several linear elements lead to him. A few objects similar in size and shape to his face help to emphasize him and to pull our eye through the rest of the photograph: the hat over his head, the shiny metal container in the upper left, the objects on the table, the hanging coat, and the hands holding a shovel to the right.

As we begin to make inferences, constructing meaning from these details, students might protest that we are just "making it up" and that everyone's opinion will be different. We do not have to arrive at a certain truth, but we must arrive at a plausible tale, carefully based on what we see. More than one narrative may be convincing, but it is unlikely that many will. And one narrative—taking into account all of the elements seen and employing convincing inferences—will prevail.

In Riis's photograph, there is a common, household table, its turned legs in need of dusting. The scrap of oilcloth on the table is so filthy that many would hesitate to eat the glistening challah sitting on it. But a tablecloth hints at civility, as does the cobbler's coat, which is cleaner than his pants (similar in condition to the hanging jacket). Perhaps he put on his better garment for his Sabbath meal, or perhaps he wished to look his best in the photograph. In any case, the jacket, his good hat hanging overhead, and the relatively expensive challah suggest that hope and pride survive in this bleak situation. On the table, another hat rests on a book, possibly a Siddur, both perhaps deposited as he returned from Shul. The function of the hanging container is unclear, but it brings our eye to the left side of the photo, where we see his shop sign. The sign is in; the work day is over. We see only one chair—perhaps he will eat alone. It is unclear if he will be joined by the person whose hands are on the shovel, who may be the janitor arrived to stoke the furnace. In any case, the tool shown as a fragment disrupts the scene's domesticity.

An interesting tension exists between the visual sophistication of the photograph and the gritty truth it portrays to the viewer. It seems as if Riis did nothing but record the facts as he encountered them. Even the moment of exposure seems to record a conversation taking place between the cobbler and someone off-camera.

Jacob Riis
Ready for Sabbath Eve in a Coal Cellar, A Cobbler on Ludlow Street
The Jacob A. Riis Collection, #286 Museum of the City of New York.
Photo: © Bettman/Corbis.

Links

Compare this image by Jacob Riis to others.

Collections of his images can be found on the website of the Museum of the City of New York at: **http://www.mcny.org/Exhibitions/riis/riis2.htm**

The hypertext edition of Riis's influential work *How the Other Half Lives* is published online at Yale University's American Studies website: **http://www.cis.yale.edu/amstud/inforev/riis/title.html**

Writer at Work

William Cronon holds the title of Frederick Jackson Turner Professor of History, Geography, and Environmental Studies at the University of Wisconsin. He is not a professional art historian; rather, he is interested in the ways that concepts of wilderness and landscape are developed and disseminated in society through texts and images. "Telling Tales on Canvas" is an excerpt from an art exhibition catalogue of paintings that were exhibited at Yale University and the Gilcrease Museum of Western Art in Tulsa, Oklahoma. In it, Cronon explores the ways that landscape painting reflected nineteenth-century American values and shaped American desires to acquire land and settle the West. As Cronon argues, sometimes it is almost impossible to separate images from **mythology**, *the mix of icons, clichés, and ideology that surrounds a particular idea. The frontier narrative is a key founding myth of the United States, an idea that the western territories were a promised land. Paintings such as those by Emanuel Gottlieb Leutze, George Catlin, and Thomas Cole persuaded people to move westward. Therefore Cronon reads the images almost as if they were advertisements.*

Freewrite

As you read "Telling Tales on Canvas," outline Cronon's analysis. Is he interested in the emotional effect of the image? Is he curious about the formal elements of the painting he studies?

As you read the excerpt below, notice that Cronon describes the genre of nineteenth-century **history** **paintings** *of the American West as if they were historical* **narratives** *or ethnographic evidence.*

Telling Tales on Canvas
Landscapes of Frontier Change
William Cronon

Among the most famous images of western American art—so famous that many no doubt regard it as a cliché—is Emanuel Leutze's mural of migrating pioneers, which decorates the U.S. Capitol building in Washington, D.C. An equally famous (and equally clichéd) line from Bishop George Berkeley's poem supplies Leutze's title: *Westward the Course of Empire Takes Its Way.* The composition assembles a hodgepodge of familiar icons to celebrate the American migration westward. Horses and riders strain to move covered wagons up steep, rocky slopes. Rifle-toting frontiersmen direct the party forward while axmen toil to clear the way ahead. As the wagons pass, a mourning family erects a cross and conducts a funeral for a loved one who will never complete the journey. And at the center of the composition is a buckskinned figure that can only be Daniel Boone reincarnated, leaning over a mother and her infant—themselves the very picture of a Raphaelite Madonna and child—while gesturing confidently toward the western horizon. Leutze clearly intended this westward gesture to express all that was most hopeful in America's manifest destiny, a vision of national progress in which the frontier experience and the dream of new lives on virgin lands would be the foundation of American unity. The optimism of the mural was all the more poignant for its having been completed in 1862, before the new Capitol was even finished, and as the bloody ordeal of national union had barely begun.

Cronon, William. "Telling Tales on Canvas: Landscapes of Frontier Change." *Discovered Lands, Invented Pasts: Transforming Visions of the America West.* Edited by Jules David Prown. Copyright © 1992, Yale University Press. Reprinted by permission of Yale University Press.

The landscape of Leutze's painting plays backdrop to the human drama in the foreground. The Boone character and his Madonna sit atop a small hillock that is echoed by a large rocky outcrop behind them, where two men have scrambled to get a better view of the way ahead. The outcrop is echoed in turn by foothills leading up toward snowcapped peaks that fill the upper right-hand quadrant of the painting, sublime sentinels looking down upon the great migration below. But the landscape that matters most to the composition lies elsewhere. Off to the west, lit by the golden light of an unseen setting sun, lies a broad flat plain with the glistening hint of an ocean beyond. Our travelers have evidently just crested a pass in the mountains and are about to make their way down to the new Canaan below. Relief and excitement illuminate every face, and if we have any doubt about the ultimate destination of this party, an inset landscape of San Francisco Bay immediately below the main composition shows us the end of the road.

Strikingly, though, Leutze's California is almost featureless. The western portion of his composition is entirely a landscape of expectation, the endpoint of a human drama in which Americans on their westward course of empire plod across the broad plains, struggle over mountain passes, and descend at last to a land of plenty. The mountains these travelers are crossing bear little resemblance to the Sierra Nevada, jumbling together instead geological shapes one might expect to find more readily in the Central Rockies or the mesa country of the Southwest. That hardly matters, of course, for in the symbolic language of the painting the mountains serve a purely narrative function. To the right, they are about the uphill battle to build a nation in the face of natural obstacles; to the left, they are about turning points, downward descents, and the rewards of journeys ending. As for the lowlands that glow like the skin of a peach in the light of the western sun, Leutze leaves to the viewer's imagination what these travelers will find when they arrive at their new home.

. . .

The Oxbow [by Thomas Cole, 1836] and *Westward the Course of Empire Takes Its Way* offer important lessons for those who would seek to trace the history of the American landscape from the visual record of contemporary artists like Thomas Cole and Leutze. They remind us of the multiple perspectives from which each such painting must be read before we can begin to understand its meaning. The most obvious information that an environmental historian might wish to extract from these paintings is what the land actually looked like at a particular time in the past. But because landscapes constantly change in response to the people who live upon them, they inevitably reflect a human telos. Even an apparently static image like Cole's describes not just its present moment but a long process of human use that has given this valley its form—a process the painting records as a kind of palimpsest. Furthermore, because so much of American landscape art has a prophetic element pointing toward national progress and its consequences, landscapes such as these also reflect the hopes and anxieties of the artists who paint them. Reading the history of environmental change from these images thus requires us to place each painting in a dynamic continuum that encompasses not just the painting's present moment but the past from which the landscape emerged and the future toward which its artist believed it was heading.

Most American landscape paintings locate themselves within a relatively small number of narrative moments, so that one can easily construct a taxonomy of the historical environments they represent. The earliest of these moments consists of what we might call "the first encounter," in which the artist tries to record for the viewer a landscape seen for the first time by European eyes. Many such images were the products of early journeys into territories previously unvisited by European or American explorers. From Sir Walter Raleigh's sixteenth-century expedition to Roanoke to the Pacific Railroad surveys of the mid-nineteenth century, the visual record was a vital adjunct to the enterprise of colonization—educating viewers who might never visit these distant lands themselves, providing information for the use of scientists and politicians, and tempting at least a few people to abandon old homes for new.

Emanuel Gottlieb Leutze (1816–1868)
Westward the Course of an Empire Takes Its Way
(mural study, U.S. Capitol) 1861 oil on canvas
Smithsonian American Art Museum, Washington, D.C. Bequest of Sara Carr Upton.
Art Resource, NY.

Rereading "Telling Tales on Canvas"

In composing his analysis of the Leutze painting, which is the first part of his extended chapter on the relationship of western art to American idealism, Cronon tells a story about the painting. Why must he use words in order to discuss the painting? Is the "story" of this history painting not evident visually?

This desire to retell the story is actually a common move in art history, especially when figures and settings are part of the story to be analyzed. (Images from the Renaissance, extending approximately from the fourteenth through seventeenth centuries, were often painted versions of biblical stories; in the eighteenth century there was a fad for paintings of scenes from Shakespeare's plays.) Narrating puts the viewer and the writer on the same ground, because the viewer now "sees" the way that the writer is interpreting the painting. At the same time, we recognize that we may have different ways of understanding an image, just as we differ in our understandings of novels, short stories, and films. The stories we tell about any image vary.

Cronon sees the painting as a narrative and thus his critical essay presents his "story" about the characters, actions, and motivations of the painting. This makes his analytical scheme different from those of Scholes and Hovanec and Freund. At the same time, some of the same techniques are used, such as the record of the formal elements of the image and the investigation of the historical context of the work. Looking closely at Cronon's narrative, we can isolate three distinct steps of analytical development: storytelling, historical context, and formal elements.

Step One: Storytelling. Cronon begins his analysis by itemizing the elements of the painting: horse, rider, covered wagon, and figures. At the center of the canvas is Daniel Boone, who Cronon indicates is the protagonist. As stories have action, Cronon ensures that he uses motion words to describe what is essentially a two-dimensional, static image: "axmen *toil*" and "wagons *pass*." The gestures of the humans are also infused with purpose, as is the direction of the figures' **gaze**. Although there is no way to prove this, Cronon speculates about what the figures in the frame see as they look beyond the frame. His speculations are rooted in history and his knowledge of **ideology**, the aspirations and beliefs of the American people in the nineteenth century as expressed in their laws, religious sermons,

> **Key Point**
>
> Cronon's Three-Point Sequence of Analysis
>
> 1. Tell the story of the image
> 2. Examine the historical context
> 3. Itemize the formal elements

newspapers, fiction, and works of art. Cronon's efforts to place the subject of the painting in a wider context are important for his discussion of the meaning of the painting (Step Two).

How would the story that Cronon tells be different if he identified a different protagonist in the painting? For a creative writing assignment, write the story of this journey from the point of view of another member of the traveling party depicted in the painting.

Step Two: Historical context. Because Cronon is setting up an argument that paintings can be understood as historical documents, it is important for him to think culturally outside the frame of the painting. By thinking culturally about the context in which the painting was created, Cronon is able to establish that the mood of America in the nineteenth century was one of optimism. National progress— building railroads, settling the areas between the Mississippi River and the Pacific Ocean, establishing a network of trade—illustrated important political and economic ideas in the century. As a painter living in that time, he argues, Leutze would have been affected by this national optimism and would have either reflected or critiqued it in his painting. That this painting is an endorsement of national ideology rather than a critique can be proved by turning to the structural details of the painting (Step Three).

If a critic were to point out that this painting obscures a darker reality in American history, what historical facts would be brought to bear as evidence? These elements are not likely to be represented in the painting itself, either physically as elements or ideologically in the painter's attitude toward his subject.

Step Three: Formal elements. Creators of images, such as photographers and painters, use a visual hierarchy of size, angle, and placement to convey attitudes toward their subject. For example, the subject of the painting is frequently placed along the center horizontal/vertical axis. The subject of the painting may be larger than all other figures in the painting. Many times, other figures in the image point to or direct their gaze to the central subject. If they look upward—or if we look upward at the subject—a sense of awe or admiration is established. Cronon indicates the importance of placing Daniel Boone, the legendary explorer and guide, at the center of the national narrative and thus the painting. The official approval for westward expansion is augmented by the inclusion of the figures of the woman and child in Boone's arms, a visual reference to the Madonna and child that seems to give divine approval to Manifest Destiny, the duty to expand the United States to all compass points.

If you were to create an image of American idealism today, what would that photograph include? Would any national heroes like Daniel Boone appear in the image? How would you arrange the compositional elements of the image (the figures, the setting) to make an argument about how we should view America?

Like Cronon, many writers begin their analyses with an initial impression that is partial, experimental, and inquiring. They then examine their works closely for details of design that support their interpretation of the image. As you can see, however, emphasizing different elements of the image—even imagining what has been eliminated from the creator's gaze—can create alternative interpretations. The three writers whose ideas are presented in this chapter all offer a reading of an image—a way of understanding its meaning—only after they have considered the time and place in which the image was produced.

We know from experience, however, that the meaning of images changes over time. What seems clever and inspiring to viewers at one point in history can seem dated, passé, even offensive at later points.

Re-Vision

The images by Riis and Leutze featured in the latter half of this chapter are making visual arguments. For this re-visioning of the images in this chapter—applying your own perceptions and perspectives—use Riis's *Ready for Sabbath Eve in a Coal Cellar*, *A Cobbler on Ludlow Street* or Leutze's *Westward the Course of Empire Takes Its Way* as your subject image text. Create a written analysis of the argument or arguments that these images are making.

An argument presents the creator's position on a particular issue. The creators of images, just like the writers of verbal texts, attempt to convince others of the idea's validity and worth by using familiar images that are known to engender a positive or negative reaction. The "syntax" or structure of the visual argument is created by combining images, image elements, and, frequently, text. We recognize this from advertisements, which attempt to persuade the public that their lives would be improved by the purchase and use of a particular product.

Use the PREWRITING QUESTIONS to help you focus your analysis as you look again at these images of the American past.

PREWRITING QUESTIONS

- **First Reactions.** When you looked at the image for the first time, what was your first reaction? Even no reaction—passing the picture by—reflects something of your attitude toward the image. If you had an emotional reaction to the image, put that into words.

- **Gaze.** What attitude does the creator of the image seem to have about the subject? For example, is Riis sympathetic toward the situation of the cobbler? Is Leutze in favor of western expansion? Could you describe the stance as positive or negative?

- **Formal Elements.** Isolate the smaller, physical elements of the image. List the materials that are represented, such as a broom or hat. Look carefully at how the figures are dressed and how they are physically positioned on the surface.

- **Historical Research.** Research something about the time that the image was created. What were the major social or political concerns of the day? How does the image draw attention to those concerns?

- **Biographical Research.** Look for information about the methods that the creator employed to create the images. For example, how did Riis find his cobbler in order to photograph him? What were some of the challenges of documentary photography at the turn of the twentieth century?

- **Audience.** Put yourself in the place of someone living at the time that the image was first displayed. What would an audience in the nineteenth century see in these images? Who is the audience now? How does time change the meaning of the image?

- **Storytelling.** Write down the story of the image. What are the characters doing and thinking? What might be their hopes, dreams, and fears?

- **Themes.** A theme is a general idea explored through language or image. Themes might be something like greed, hope, or desire. *Westward the Course of Empire Takes Its Way* is an idealistic painting. What are some of the American themes that the painting offers the viewer? What themes does Riis explore with his camera?

In Focus: Images and Analysis

For this IN FOCUS writing and visual display assignment, find your own images that make arguments. You will be composing an essay in which you argue for a particular interpretation of the images. The images you select may be purely visual or may use text. Some good texts to use for investigation are advertisements, real estate notices, book covers, posters for performing events, recruiting posters for organizations or societies, and daily cartoon strips like *Doonesbury* or *The Boondocks*. Begin your analysis by noting your first impressions of the text, then dig deeper. What are the images arguing? What is the attitude of the creator toward the subject matter (sympathy, endorsement, critique)? What is the image's purpose? Where was it published or disseminated? Who is the audience? Do the text and image augment each other or does the text contradict the image? How might a slightly different image change the meaning of the text? Use this project as the basis of a classroom presentation on the persuasive qualities of images.

On Display: Peter Pan

In this essay, you will compare two illustrations of a popular children's book character: Peter Pan.

From an early age, at school or at home, we learn about the world through pictures. Picture books teach us the alphabet, how to count, or about concepts like "weather." As we advance in years, although pictures begin to decrease in size and frequency in the texts we read, we never quite lose sight of book illustrations. The covers, endpapers, title pages, and spines of textbooks, novels, magazines, and handbooks often contain some illustration. Computer manuals, home improvement and decorating handbooks, gardening books, travel guides, and cookbooks all contain illustrations. Children's book author Welleran Poltarnees writes that book illustrations have three discernable relationships to the words of the books:

1. They show things described in words by the authors. The book illustrations offer demonstration.

2. They show things mentioned in the text, but not described. The illustrations augment or extend the text from the author's world to that of the illustrator's imagination.

3. They show things neither mentioned nor described by the authors. The artist has a full range of creative liberty to interpret the meaning of the text for the audience.

A continuously popular figure in American culture is the boy hero Peter Pan. First created by author J. M. Barrie in 1902 in a book titled

The Little White Bird, the boy has been represented on stage, screen, and in books by actors and illustrators. Yet, in the novel *Peter Pan,* only one line describes the boy: "He was a lovely boy, clad in skeleton leaves and the juices that ooze out of trees; but the most entrancing thing about him was that he had all his first teeth." Use Poltarnees's criteria to initiate a comparison of these two illustrations of the boy Peter Pan. You may find yourself remembering and consulting the famous film versions of the novel, such as the 1953 Disney movie, to augment your investigation.

Peter Pan
© 1940. Charles Scribner's Sons. Illustrated by Edmund Blampied.

Peter Pan

Reprinted with the permission of Atheneum Books for Young
Readers, an imprint of Simon and Schuster Children's Publishing
Division from *Peter Pan* by J. M. Barrie, pictures by Trina Schart
Hyman. Illustrations copyright © 1980 Trina Schart Hyman.

2

The Elements of
Critical Viewing

A New Language

As Chapter One set forth, the term **visual culture** applies to the world of visual expression and the history of visual representations. In the first chapter, the arts of cartooning, photography, and painting were emphasized. We know, however, that there are many other forms of visual expression. Each visual image or each object that we respond to visually uses certain elements of design to convey its message. In this chapter, you will discover ways to make a careful accounting of the elements of an image.

When you look at a family photograph, an image in an advertisement, or a poster on a coffee shop wall, what do you see? How might you turn your initial positive or negative reaction into a critical process of analysis? Critical viewing entails looking closely at an image to comprehend its structure and to evaluate the information presented. "What you see is a major part of what you know," writes Donis Dondis, author of a popular visual studies handbook. Our goal is to move from being passive consumers of images to active interrogators. This takes study. Initially, if possible, we should think consensually and sympathetically, reading the image in the way that it appears to be intended to be read, avoiding critique until after we examine the elements of the image. This process involves a degree of intellectual largesse on our part, meaning that we grant to the author of the image our attempt to understand his or her judgments, even if we disagree. Thinking consensually is not always possible, especially when we view images of war, strife, and privation, because the images cause us to react with horror and outrage. Yet, our repulsion can be an agent for meaningful change as we seek to investigate the conditions under which images were created and disseminated.

For example, in late April of 2004, snapshots of Iraqi prisoners of war at the Abu Ghraib prison near Baghdad were released to the American press. Apparently taken by the American soldiers responsible for the interrogation of the prisoners, the photos showed the prisoners in humiliating and demeaning postures as the soldiers looked on, smiling. These images were difficult to look at because of their high emotional content, and a consensual stance toward the imagemakers was not easy to come by; nonetheless, the rhetorical question of what purpose the photographs served leads to crucial questions. Personal war images, either snapshots or sketches, are not unique to the Iraqi war. Were the images taken to coerce admissions during interrogation? Was each taken with the same purpose in mind? Were any of the photos individualized as a *souvenir de guerre*—a memento of war—for the personal archives of the individual soldiers? What conditions led to the photos being taken?

Even though we begin by examining what the creator may have intended, we need to keep in mind that there is never a single interpretation of an image, so our goal is not to discover the right interpretation, but to offer potential readings of an image. As Rebecca Platzner and Kay Vandergrift write about analyzing children's picture books, "meaning is created as the result of a transaction between an individual reader and a text at a specific moment in time . . . it follows that there will be many possible interpretations of any text or illustration." Images can also form the basis of a transaction between people. Advertising does this regularly by conveying a message to many readers. When you see an image that you like or dislike, show it to a friend and ask what they see in it.

The goal of this chapter is to help you establish a process and develop a language for examining

> **Discuss**
>
> Share images with friends and family to discover what others see and how they react. You may be surprised!

visual images. You not only want to describe what is there before you, you also want to understand why the creator made certain choices. Sylvan Barnett, the author of several texts on analyzing fine art, writes that we "see" with more than our eyes: when we look at objects and images, we engage emotions, memory, and ideology (the system of values and beliefs into which we have been educated).

Before continuing with your work, remember two things. First, whenever possible, try to see images in their original contexts. While digital technology has made it possible for many art galleries, museums, and image lovers to put high-quality color images of paintings, photographs, and sculpture online, they all appear on the same small, flat screen. Missing is the context of viewing: the hushed tones of the art museum or the buzz of the coffee house. These ambient noises contribute to our mood and, when viewing the images before us, our mood can lead us to make certain decisions about the image. In addition, if your subject is painting, there is no reproduction that can enable you to experience the texture of thick paint on canvas, such as the daubs of a fine brush that made the painting

A Sunday on La Grande Jatte (1884) by French painter Georges Seurat so famous. Its sheer size is another compelling reason to visit this painting at its home in the Art Institute of Chicago. That the painting is life sized makes those tiny dabs of green, red, and blue on the surface of the canvas all the more amazing.

> **Key Point**
>
> Try to look at images in their original contexts, whether museum, magazine, or family album.
>
> Initially read images without any accompanying text.

Second, remember that, if you are working with images accompanied by text, you should try to read the images without the text in order to discover what message the illustrator was trying to convey. As we saw in Chapter One, even media such as cartoons that habitually join text and image still rely on conventions of image production to make sense. Sometimes, text and images work independently, even though they may be joined. At times, the image may contradict the text—or the text may contradict the image. Barbie Zelizer points out in her exploration of World War II photography that images of concentration camps were often misidentified by caption writers. Working in America, far away from the atrocious camps, the photoeditors at newspapers were interested in broadly conveying the horror of the camp conditions in Germany, Poland, and Czechoslovakia; they were less interested in specifically identifying the name of the camp, its location, or the names and nationalities of the human subjects in the camera's eye. Only in later decades, when historians

> **Links**
>
> Excellent collections of historical images may be found online at the Library of Congress's American Memory Project, **memory.loc.gov/ammem**

began to reassemble the records of incarceration, did the need to verbally identify all the elements of the images become crucial.

Step-by-Step Analysis

There are nine steps to follow in this chapter. Each of the steps of critical viewing can be isolated from the others; you can write an analysis using only one or two of these steps. However, they are arranged to proceed in a logical process from initial reaction through research into the life of the creator and into the technical procedures used to create the image. In addition, the steps are **recursive**: they can be returned to at different points in the process of analysis. William Cronon used a protocol very similar to the one outlined below in his analysis of the painting *Westward the Course of Empire Takes its Way* (Chapter One).

Step One	Record your initial impression.
Step Two	Place the image in context.
Step Three	Describe the image in detail (visual discrimination).
Step Four	Identify symbolic elements.
Step Five	Distinguish absences.
Step Six	Examine the self as a viewer of images (exploring the horizon of expectations).
Step Seven	Consider the effect of the image on the viewer (visual communication).
Step Eight	Research the image.
Step Nine	Prepare an interpretation.

Step One: Record Your Initial Impression

Every time we look at images, whether they are book jackets, advertisements, street signs, posters, billboards, or photographs in the newspaper, we immediately have a reaction. The image either compels us to examine it closer or to look away. Sometimes it is the subject of the image that draws us in. A sumptuous chocolate cake on the cover of a cooking magazine may make us buy the magazine so that we can make (and eat) the cake. Sometimes the image is unfamiliar and we look closer to find out what is happening. In the first year of the war with Iraq, news images of U.S. troops interacting with Iraqi men and women made us look closer at the images and read the captions to determine whether the encounters between Americans and Iraqis were (even temporarily) amicable or hostile.

> **Freewrite**
>
> Make a list of objects or concepts that elicit good feelings (warm reactions), such as *sunsets, home,* and *mother.*

If we are fascinated by a celebrity such as Britain's Prince William, we may be drawn to pick up a supermarket tabloid and page through it while we wait in line with our purchases. Advertisers and magazine publishers depend on "warm," or sympathetic, reactions from patrons to sell their products.

Yet we also have reactions, good or bad, to images that are not strictly commercial. The novel you are asked to purchase for your English class may have an image on the cover. If it is a classic work of literature, the image may be drawn from historical painting. If the novel is contemporary, it may have an abstract image on the cover, or even a photograph of the author. These images lead us to believe that we may want to read the book or initially convince us that the text between the covers is alien to our experiences.

A recent example of a book cover that was redesigned for different readership is the cover for the British edition of the first book in the *Harry Potter* series, *Harry Potter and the Philosopher's Stone,* by J. K. Rowling. (The British edition uses a different title than the American edition.) The first copies of *Harry Potter and the Philosopher's Stone* were designed for children and used a colorful, cartoonish illustration of the hero Harry near the train that would take him to wizarding school, the Hogwarts Express. Once the book became a best-seller, the publisher discovered that adults were curious about the novel, but were somewhat reluctant to be seen reading a text with an illustrated cover. Consequently, they reissued the novel with a new cover, a black-and-white photograph of an ominous-looking locomotive traversing an urban landscape, billowing a cloud of black smoke. The tone of the cover changed from lighthearted and magical to dark and foreboding. If you are interested in this topic, search used bookstores, libraries, and the Internet for different editions of the same novel and compare their cover illustrations. The older the book, the more variety you will find in the covers, as they change across time.

> ## Links
>
> Compare cover images for the book *Harry Potter and the Sorcerer's Stone* by visiting **Amazon.com** (USA) and **Amazon.com.co.uk** (Great Britain). When searching for the book in Great Britain, make sure you use its original English title, *Harry Potter and the Philosopher's Stone.*

Step Two: Place the Image in Context

Each image is developed from the knowledge and resources of a historical moment. The availability of materials at a particular time, in a certain geographic location provides a means of expression. Similarly, the audience, once familiar with certain standards of image production, comes to judge future images by comparing them to existing standards. As you conduct an analysis, you will want to take into consideration the time and place in which the image was created. This will mean that you socially situate the image in a context that is greater than just you looking closely.

The basic questions for contextual analysis are:

Who created the image?

When was it created?

Where was it originally published and displayed?

Who was the intended and initial audience?

What medium is the image created from?

Is there a title or caption that explains the subject of the image (or confounds explanation)?

What is the subject of the image?

What was the original purpose in creating and displaying the image?

You may be able to answer many of these questions by simply looking closely. If you are studying an advertisement for an automobile in *Time* or *Wired* magazine, you will be able to answer that the creator of the image is the car manufacturer who hired a photographer and a team of artists to create this image. Generally, advertisements are not associated with specific names of artists or photographers in the way that a fine art image such as an artistic photograph is associated with a name such as "Ansel Adams" or the way that an oil painting commands high respect (and prices) by having the name "Winslow Homer" on its canvas.

Because advertisements are concerned with selling the most up-to-date products, the advertising images were created close to the time of printing. The text in the advertisement also provides clues, by tying into current language, styles, and societal knowledge. If there is no text with the image other than the name of the manufacturer, we would need to look at other visual cues to date the image. Assuming that the image is removed from the pages of a dated magazine—as sometimes happens when the image is reproduced in a textbook or scholarly edition—we would have to think about car design, architectural styles, and even (if we look closely at the models who may be featured) a knowledge of hairstyles and clothing design. From our recognition of these elements, we can date the photograph as "recent"

> **Freewrite**
>
> What are some current fashions that could be represented visually in advertisements? Are there any slang terms or spellings that you might expect to see in ads?

or "historical," even if we are not completely certain when it initially appeared. These visual cues operate continuously and allow us to make decisions about whether something is contemporary with our present experience or whether it is an image from the past. Many advertisers and product designers adopt older (what we might call "retro") visual styles. Developing a familiarity with the visual styles of different eras may also be useful to our analysis.

In considering where the image was published, keep in mind that images—especially those in magazines and newspapers—travel from location to location. The context in which an image is viewed includes whether you sight it on the newsstand at the supermarket or have the publication delivered to your home; whether you are browsing the magazine in a dentist's office or whether you have taken it into your bed because you are sick with a cold and want to divert your attention. Images are portable: they move between public and private worlds with ease, and often regardless of the original intention of the creator.

A slick double-paged magazine advertisement is created from film, digitized computer files, ink, and paper. Even though we recognize that most advertisements use photographs (rather than, say, watercolor, finger paint, or cut-paper), we might not know the extent to which the image has been digitally managed by computer photoediting software such as Adobe PhotoShop. On a simple scale, we recognize that there may be manipulation in an ad for diet pills in which the now-slender woman holds up a pair of size twenty pants that the text claims were once hers. However, we may not recognize the degree to which apparently realistic scenes are adjusted by photoenhancement tools that add sheen and depth, that replace backgrounds and even bodies. The "truth" of the advertisement may be created by photoeditors working in a studio.

In searching for the title of the work or the caption of the advertisement, you may find several. A literal caption is designed to identify and classify the type of product pictured so that the reader may develop brand recognition. Other text uses persuasive language that makes the claims for an improved life that the product will offer. As you look at advertisements, separate the identification of the product from the persuasive language of the copy. How does the text enhance or support the image?

Step Three: Describe the Image in Detail

Describing the image in detail allows us to focus on the way that the image has been put together by the creator. As viewers ("readers") of the image, we should be able to conduct a close reading of many elements of the image, such as color, shape, and contrast. The arrangement of all the parts is called the composition of the image. In other words, we develop a vocabulary that allows us to **discriminate**, to make distinctions between different elements that compose the whole.

All images engage formal elements of composition, meaning that they have a certain form for a certain reason. Artists work with seven basic **Elements of Design: color, value**, line, shape, form, texture, and space. Art historians who engage in **formal** (or "formalist") criticism study the arrangement of certain elements in a painting or sculpture such as the placement of an image of Jesus in religious art of the Renaissance. Their interest is in the design and arrangement of elements rather than in the content (the subject and meaning) of the image. With this approach, a Renaissance altar piece of Jesus on the cross would be evaluated in a similar way to an abstract painting by Jackson Pollock. While formalist *criticism* is one way to examine an image, a good formal *analysis* of the elements of the composition underlies all forms of criticism, from the psychological to the deconstructive.

As you look closely at images, you can inventory, first, the **literal elements** of the image (Elements of Design), such as gradients of color and shadow; second, you can discuss the **arrangement** (Principles of Design) of the individual elements of the image.

One way to begin a formal analysis is to create a chart and fill in the blanks with notes that you write as you look at an image. This provides you with a list of design elements, the literal qualities of the image.

Elements of Design: Literal Elements

Literal Elements	Definitions
Color	Colors are identified by name, hue, tint, or intensity. Color schemes include primary colors (red, yellow, blue), secondary colors (orange, green, violet), and tertiary colors (the uneven mixture of primary colors). Color schemes can be warm (reds and oranges) or cool (blues).
Value	Particularly important when studying black-and-white images, *value* refers to lightness or darkness of color. The degree to which the image is given depth by shadows can also be considered here.

Literal Elements	Definitions
Line	A mark made by an instrument such as a pencil, pen, or brush creates a line. Its direction may be identified as horizontal, vertical, or diagonal. Lines can be thick or thin, sharp or blurred, curved or straight.
Shape	The outline or external contour of an object can be traced to find its shape. The term also refers to geometric figures such as the oval, circle, or square. Shape may be represented directly or implied by the arrangement of objects.
Form	Primarily an element of three-dimensional works, *form* refers to volume (height, width, and depth).
Texture	The surface of an object may be real (as in fabric) or simulated (as in a painting or photo). Surface qualities are described as rough, smooth, bumpy, etc.
Space	The distance between objects, the area around an object, or the open areas inside a three-dimensional object creates space. Space can be two-dimensional (suggested by outlines in a painting or photograph) or three-dimensional (created by form as in sculpture).

While all images have literal elements, they cannot have meaning beyond pure form without an arrangement into a sequence or series of relationships that mimic reality. Abstract art is given meaning by its literal elements of form; however, a family photograph, a photograph in an advertisement, or a painting of shepherds in a field consists of an arrangement of the elements that tell a story, create an emotion, or make an argument. The arrangement of the elements into a form that provides meaning is referred to as **Principles of Design**.

Principles of Design: Arrangement

Arrangement	Definitions
Perspective	A system of arrangement in two-dimensional works that creates the illusion of distance, depth, and proportion.
Angle, Vantage Point, Point of View	The relationship of the viewer to the image. Spectators look on the scene or object from above, below, outside, or inside.
Framing	Beyond the familiar physical object, a frame is a pictorial concept in which one object inside the area of the image encloses another, thereby drawing attention to the second object.
Dominance (emphasis)	Weight, line, shape, texture, and color all bring objects to the fore, or allow them to recede into the background. The dominant items are emphasized as being important to the meaning of the image.
Balance	The harmonious position of objects in the image, frequently brought about because of the symmetrical arrangement of similar or complementary elements.
Proportion	The compatible relationship between objects of the same size and weight.
Pattern	The repetition of elements in an image.
Contrast	A significant difference between objects, colors, or other elements of the image is used for emphasis.
Grid	Intersecting horizontal or vertical lines that cross the surface of the image suggest or actually inscribe a grid. A center point (or dividing line) may create mirrored halves that pattern the image.

The key element of arrangement is perspective. The term perspective refers to a system of lines and proportions that creates the illusion of a three-dimensional surface on a two-dimensional object. One of the principal means of creating perspective is through the manipulation of the size of objects, called **proportion**. An object that is larger and placed in the foreground of an image is understood by viewers to be closer to them than a smaller-sized object placed along a plane in the background. An obvious representation of how perspective depends on a series of lines to create the illusion of receding space and depth is the image of railroad tracks. In this image, the buildings on the plane in the background are miniscule when compared to the train car on the right.

The parallel lines of the tracks appear to converge as they recede toward the **vanishing point** on the **horizon line**. The invisible lines that converge on the horizon line (the invisible horizontal line that marks the division between earth and sky) are called **orthogonal** lines.

Perspective is not a natural system, but one that was developed as a theory in the fifteenth century. Not all images use perspective. Some use a series of converging or overlapping planes. A **plane** is a flat surface or an area within the field of vision. Planes may be divided into foreground, middle ground, and background. Artists such as Picasso worked with the effects of planes during the Cubist period. This image of a beach is essentially two planes: the sky and the water, divided by the horizon line, where the sea and sky appear to meet.

Another compositional technique used to place objects on the picture plane is that of an imagined or inscribed **grid** of intersecting horizontal and vertical lines. The center of the image may be placed at the center of the grid. Often, a **dividing line** is implied or inscribed and the images are mirrored on either side of that center point. The grid offers a flatter image surface than the perspective system, but it is used often in advertising as a means of laying out the interrelated elements of text and design.

When you look at an image, you will come to see that you are placed in a relationship to the image. In general, you are outside, looking in, as if through a window. Sometimes, however, the subjects of the image directly address you, looking up from their activity as if to ask you a question or invite you into their world. Famous paintings invite us in, such as Diego Velasquez's *Las Meninas* (1657), Joseph Wright of Derby's *An Experiment on a Bird in the Airpump* (1768), and Charles Willson Peale's self-portrait known as *The Artist in His Museum* (1822).

As we look at a picture, a number of different **points of view** are possible: we may gaze from above, below, or outside or be enveloped in the action on the inside. The direction in which we look is represented by angles on the picture plane; however, we also metaphorically call the direction of our gaze the **angle** from which we view a picture. Another term is **vantage point**. If you have

Links

Visit the Web Museum to find digital images of these famous paintings by Velasquez and Wright: **www.ibiblio.org/wm/**

An image of Peale's painting can be found at the Pennsylvania Academy of Fine Arts: **www.pafa.org**

ever stopped to take a picture of a building that towers above you such as a cathedral or skyscraper, you will turn your camera upward to catch the image. The building will angle upward in your photograph; your vantage point as a viewer of that photograph will place you below the subject (see the figure below for an example). Most family photographs are taken so that the subjects look straight ahead at us (see the figure on page 89 for an example). Our vantage point is on an even plane, symbolically placing us on an equal footing with the object. Many monuments are created so that

we look up at them; our posture places us in a position of reverence and awe toward the monument.

Sometimes, in advertisements or in fine art, images are framed in order to direct the eye to the focal point. In this sense, the frame is not a physical object made of wood or metal (such as the picture frames that you have around your snapshots at home), but a construction within the image itself. In this image, the frame of the doorway forces the eye inward toward the courtyard.

In images, certain visual ideas come to the fore, either through their perceived **weight** (using line, shape, and texture) or through their **color**. The **dominance** of particular visual elements gives the picture meaning. A prevalence of black in an image, for example, usually connotes death.

If an object is large, taking up the entire frame, its dominance indicates its importance to the meaning of the image.

Ideas are also conveyed to an audience through **balance**, **proportion, pattern**, and **contrast**. While each of these terms has its own definition, they often cross-reference each other. For example, a balanced image gives the viewer a sense of harmony because of the pleasing repetition of shapes or forms in the image. The weight or dominance of these repeated elements unifies the image. Balance may be **symmetrical** (one side repeats the elements of the other side), **asymmetrical** (each side contains different elements, but uses the same weight), or **radial** (using a circle as a design template). Many artists use reflections in water or mirrors to create patterns and symmetry, arranging the parts along a dividing line. If something is balanced, it is also usually proportionate, meaning that the size of the elements and the quantity of the elements are measured according to the standards of perspective and customs of representing physical objects and space in the world.

Balanced images often make use of pattern—repeated images, shapes, colors, or lines—to create a meaning. At the same time, many images convey meaning by using contrast. A good example of contrast in an image is the placing of something old next to something new. Contrast also occurs when colors are altered or when light and dark intersect for effect.

Step Four: Identify Symbolic Elements

In an influential book called *A Primer of Visual Literacy*, author Donis Dondis proposes that visual information is processed on three levels: **representational, abstract**, and **symbolic**. Representational information is recognizable as something found in the environment (we sometimes call this "realism"). Abstract information is reduced to elemental components such as geometry, line, and color. Symbolic information takes the form of conventional systems of communication in which humans have constructed signs and attached meaning to them. The alphabet and the number systems we use employ symbols. The curved symbol for the numeral 2, for example, does not replicate something found in nature, but expresses a concept about groups of things such as sheep, candles, or people.

> **Key Point**
> Images may be representational, abstract, or symbolic.

As Dondis writes, symbols require "ultimate simplicity, the reduction of visual detail to the irreducible minimum." Symbols need to be immediately understood, remembered, and replicated. The use of symbols to represent ideas is called **iconography**, from *eikon*, meaning "symbol," and *graph*, meaning "writing." Historically, many societies in Europe, South America, North America, Australia, and Asia used icons to represent transactions and record history. Cave paintings of buffalo and horses used symbols to communicate messages about hunting grounds or to celebrate animal gods.

In modern society, traffic signs and restroom signs perform the same function of communication, either aiding the reader or providing a warning. Corporations and organizations use icons to advertise their products or announce their services. Perhaps the most famous icon of the American road is the twin golden arches of McDonald's. Icons that individuals and groups come to use are often highly abstract and frequently depend on cultural contexts to be fully understood. For this reason, certain icons and images that were created in other countries or in earlier decades can be unintelligible to modern American viewers.

> **Discuss**
>
> Bring in examples of modern product or corporate icons to share with the class. Do you see a relationship between the shape of the icon and the concept it is meant to represent?

Secret societies or sects such as the Freemasons, Jewish Kabbalists (who perceive the divine name of God in Hebrew letterforms), and modern graffiti artists also use icons. In their survey of icons and symbols, Rosemary Sassoon and Albertine Gaur suggest six possible uses for icons in contemporary society:

1. To make a mark on the world, as in a signature
2. To communicate when alphabetic or numeric systems fail
3. To converse with those who do not understand our language
4. To initiate a story
5. To project our image (here understood as an idea about the self) onto others
6. To offer information that needs to be quickly understood

In the Middle Ages and the Renaissance, a complex visual language of symbols was used by painters and book illustrators (who were called **illuminators**). This language is called "iconography," or writing (*graph*) with symbols (*icons*). Today, some of the same meanings of the symbols are likely to survive; for example, the circle maintains a symbolic meaning in Western society as an image of unity. However, our contemporary icons are more likely commercial shorthand, such as the Nike swoosh.

When we discuss the symbolic content of images, though, we are not just dealing with iconography, but with a complex psychological system of meaning. One of the reasons that images are used so prevalently in American society is that they carry intellectual and emotional content. A photograph used in an advertisement is not merely a display of the product, but often is an argument about how we should live our lives. Similarly, a snapshot of a vacation in a family album is not merely an image of the beach or a mountain camp, but a memory of a pleasant past time. We can say, then, that while images are composed of literal elements, they also have a symbolic quality that contructs their meaning.

> **Freewrite**
>
> Alone or with the class, brainstorm on the ways that the following advertising subjects attempt to persuade us of particular societal values: alcohol, cars, cleaning products.

Taking the idea of symbolism a step further, certain images consciously employ recognizable symbols that add to their meaning. Before we begin hunting down all the potential symbols in an image, however, we need to ask whether the creator left clues that this work was to be taken symbolically. Some clues may be the subject (a religious work is certainly symbolic) or the title (a university logo that shows a tree can be taken symbolically to mean that it represents the tree of knowledge). Principles of design such as dominance or elements such as color also suggest that the work has a symbolic content.

Although there are many more possible symbols and meanings than those listed here, this short list of common symbols and the ideas that they represent should help you begin to think about the meanings applied to ordinary objects:

Book	Knowledge, wisdom
Circle	Totality, wholeness, seasonal cycles
Cross	Christian symbol of redemption; also, the tree of life
Dog	Loyalty, vigilance
Keys	Keys to heaven in Christianity; liberation or confinement
Moon	Femininity, the unconscious, the phases of life
Skull	The mutability of life, but also the indestructibility of life
Sun	Power, universality
Tree	Life, knowledge

In addition, the use or dominance of particular colors has symbolic meaning. Red can mean passion or anger. Yellow often connotes joy and optimism. Blue, commonly used in flags, frequently means loyalty. Green, the color of spring leaves and grasses, denotes renewal and fertility. Black is the color of death, mourning, and mystery.

Often, though, color is used in ways that are less symbolic. Colors may underscore the setting, season, or personality of the subject of the image. A man or woman seated in a subtly decorated, elegant restaurant wearing a large purple-feathered boa around an orange sweater may indicate the displacement of this guest in this location. While the color choice is startling, it is less of a symbol for royalty (purple) or enthusiasm (orange) than a comment on identity, personal style, and contextual expectations.

Links

Search the following websites for images:

Washington Crossing the Delaware: the Metropolitan Museum of Art: **www.metmuseum.org**

Mona Lisa and *The Last Supper:* WebMuseum: **www.ibiblio.org/wm/**

Pieta, The Artchive: **Artchive.com**

"I want you for the US Army," The Library of Congress Online Exhibitions pages: **www.loc.gov/exhibits/**

Finally, images can also be symbolic when they allude to other works: Emanuel Gottlieb Leutze's *Washington Crossing the Delaware* (1851), Leonardo Da Vinci's *Mona Lisa* (circa 1503) and *The Last Supper* (1498), Michaelangelo's *Pieta* (1499), and James Montgomery Flagg's World War I recruiting poster of Uncle Sam ("I want you for the US Army," 1917) are all images that have been borrowed or parodied. This process is called **intertextuality** or **transtextuality**. These terms refer to the ways that images refer to each other and in so doing, cause viewers to rethink the meaning of the original as well as the imitation.

Step Five: Distinguish Absences

Images are so prevalent and persuasive that, even after identifying all the literal and symbolic elements of them, we may still not be aware that they contain significant **absences**. The theory of analyzing absence is called **deconstruction**. Deconstruction emerged as a critical force in the late 1960s from the work of French philosopher Jacques Derrida. Derrida asserted that when we read, we understand what is being told to us by setting those words and ideas against their opposites. A well-known example is that we understand the meaning of *man* in part

> **Key Point**
> Read against the grain to examine what is absent from an image. What don't you see and why?

because *man* is *not woman*. But deconstruction asks readers to press this point and ask, in effect, "Why not *woman*?" Does the absence of *woman* reveal a bias on the part of the creator? Is the author attempting to manipulate us by showing us *man* and not *woman*?

This theory of reading for absence has been called "reading against the grain." All texts, visual and verbal, have **manifest content**, that which is immediately evident and shows us what the creators wanted us to see. When we read against the grain, we read for **latent content**, that which reveals the prejudices or biases of the creators or demonstrates unconscious misgivings about the subjects. In the arts and humanities, it has been used to investigate the stories and cultural contributions of African Americans, Asian Americans, Native Americans, and members of the working class; in literature, to open up the range of works studied in the literary canon; and in media studies, to ensure equal representation on television news and entertainment programming.

What don't we see and why? What is at the margins of the picture and why? A good example of how we might use this line of inquiry to deconstruct images is to interrogate tourist brochures and vacation photography. Opening the travel section of the newspaper, you will find many ads for sunny vacation spots in the Caribbean. The residents of the Caribbean Islands, including the Bahamas, Jamaica, Cuba, Aruba, and Puerto Rico, are a diverse group of people who trace their ancestry to Africa, France, and Spain. As residents of the Islands, however, they are rarely shown in advertisements, unless it is to emphasize how ready they are to serve the typically white, fit, and middle-class visitor. Because the people in print advertisements for cruise lines and special airline packages are meant to represent the American consumer, who envisions himself or herself in the scene, the advertisements generally emphasize the activities of nonresidents, the visitors who use the islands for pleasure. These visitors take advantage of the sun, the water, the beach, and the services provided by the residents. The young visiting couples (who are constructed visually without children present and as heterosexual couples) enjoy leisure activities such as lounging on a pure white sand beach or preparing to snorkel (they are rarely in the midst of physical activity). Their adventure into the Caribbean is an escape from the cooler weather, urban sprawl, and workaday cares of their American city.

> **Discuss**
>
> Go to a travel office for brochures, look at the travel section of the newspaper, or purchase a glossy travel magazine such as *Travel & Leisure*. Examine the images for the social class, ethnicity, and gender of the people represented. What activities are the tourists engaged in?

Arguably, these images are meant to portray and purvey a fantasy and should not be examined as documentary evidence about life in the Caribbean. However, in order for the young, white, middle-class, heterosexual couple to enjoy their quick trip to the exotic and sunny south, they must depend on the work of the local residents, who cook the meals in the hotels, clean the hotel rooms and pools and wash the dishes, and make sure that the hotels are supplied with water and electricity. That the workers are often Afro-Caribbean is also significant. The manifest content of the advertisements privileges white, middle-class experience. The latent content of the image tells us that people of African descent are not privileged to take part in leisure activities either as workers, residents, or consumers.

Our own photography reveals certain biases toward leaving things out as well. This image of a picturesque cottage in northern England, for example, conforms to various standards of tourist photography: there are no people to intrude upon the scene (which might "date" the scene or destroy its visual purity) and the subject of the photograph is something *historic* (rather than the Burger King on High Street). The cottage is in fact Dove Cottage, the home of the nineteenth-century English poet William Wordsworth, and it is thus already marked as a "significant" sight for the tourist. What is missing from this image is any acknowledgment that this building represented the lived experience of inhabitants. The picture is abstract, representing American ideas about England and Englishness. The photo confirms our notions of what a "typical" English cottage should look like and that we were able to witness this traditional scene. Still influencing our tastes today, the guidelines set forward for picturesque imagery in the eighteenth century often stressed the degree to which writers and painters should include rustic elements such as cottages, gates, bending trees, and ruins. For example, to the picturesque artist, a cottage was often a better choice than a mansion. Over a century ago, British novelist George Eliot, writing in her socially conscious novel *Middlemarch* (1871), critiqued her countrymen for their failure to recognize poverty and deprivation in the midst of picturesque ruin:

> It is true that an observer, under that softening influence of the fine arts which makes other people's hardships picturesque, might have been delighted with this homestead called Freeman's End: the old house had dormer-windows in the dark-red roof, two of the chimneys were choked with ivy, the large porch was blocked up with bundles of sticks, and half the windows were closed with grey-worm-eaten shutters about which the jasmine-boughs grew in wild luxuriance; the mouldering garden wall with hollyhocks peeping over it was a perfect study of highly-minded subdued colour, and there was an aged goat (kept doubtless on interesting superstitious grounds) lying against the open back-kitchen door. The mossy thatch of the cowshed, the broken grey barn-doors, the pauper labourers in ragged breeches who had nearly finished unloading a wagon of corn into the barn ready for early thrashing; the scanty dairy of cows being tethered for milking and leaving one half of the shed in brown emptiness; the very pigs and white ducks seeming to wander about the uneven neglected yard as if in low spirits from feeding on a too meager quality of rinsing—all these objects under the quiet light of a sky marbled with high clouds would have made a sort of picture which we have all paused over as a "charming bit," touching other sensibilities than those which are stirred by the depression of the agricultural interest, with the sad lack of farming capital, as seen constantly in the newspapers of that time.

Eliot demonstrates her awareness of the conventions of the picturesque while critiquing the consequences of erasing the knowledge of actual hardship. Thus, when reading images, we must consistently remind ourselves to read against the grain, to pursue the meanings latent in the content of the image, to speak of what is not visible.

Step Six: Examine the Self as a Viewer of Images

One reason that we find ourselves looking at particular kinds of pictures is personal preference. Preferences are not natural (we are not born with particular dispositions toward, say, French Impressionist paintings of the late nineteenth century), but are learned. Our knowledge and biases are socially constructed from a host of influences: parents, teachers, friends, and the media. Too often, though, we become accustomed to tacitly acknowledging received notions of beauty. Imagine saying a sunset is ugly or that you hate bouquets of roses!

It is difficult to work against the grain and challenge ourselves to see things differently, because so many aspects of visual understanding in our society rely on the same codes: balance, symmetry, conventions of beauty, even moral codes about what is proper to display in public. Without realizing it, we approach each visual or verbal event with what literary critic Hans Robert Jauss termed a "horizon of expectations," a mental construct of what is possible or desirable for particular situations. And most of looking closely is not changing our behavior but learning to understand our own behavior better.

One of the clearest examples of how we approach images with inherent biases is that of abstract art, such as the works of Jackson Pollock or Mark Rothko. Pollock's canvases are wild, colorful, paint-spattered abstractions, while Rothko's works are elemental and planar. The work of these painters often appears to viewers to be overly simple. Many viewers say, "I could do that." What conditions some viewers to refuse to designate these works "art"? This is the question that must be investigated, in addition to the study of the work's conception, execution, and history.

Therefore, before you move on to the stage of interpreting an image, take a careful inventory of your own biases, preferences, and knowledge. Compare the self-inventory with the subject, the literal elements, and the design principles of the image. Perhaps you will notice a disjuncture or confirmation between the elements that helps explain why the image has prompted a reaction in you that is startling or pleasing.

Step Seven: Consider the Image's Effect on the Viewer

Not altogether separate from our self-inventory is the consideration of how the literal elements of the image affect us. While creators of images employ color, shape, line, and texture to communicate certain meanings, readers interpret those meanings based on their cultural position and personal experiences. We call this **affect**. Affect theory describes the psychology of emotions that are prompted by images or words. Our memories of similar images combine with the present image in order for an image to have an effect on our emotional state (in other words, in order for us to be angered or interested). Thus, affect is not purely immediate, but involves a history and pattern of response.

For example, conventional wisdom tells us that red roses are beautiful. We might recite the lines from Robert Burns's poem, "My love is like a red, red rose." Yet, Jemima Shore, a sleuth in Antonia Frazer's series of murder mysteries, abhors red flowers of all kinds because they remind her too greatly of blood. She draws from her memory of unpleasant events to interpret the flowers and their color. The effect upon her of a gift of red flowers is disgust rather than pleasure. Contemporary film director M. Night Shyamalan played on the association of the color red with blood and violence to create an element of fear in his thriller *The Village* (2004). Residents of the village are not allowed to wear red, hold red flowers, or use red to decorate their homes. By the rules of the village, it is "the forbidden color."

> **Freewrite**
>
> Quickly write down your own "history of emotions" with any of these concepts and images:
>
> Flag
>
> Flower
>
> Dog
>
> Cat
>
> Sunset
>
> Picnic
>
> Dance

Step Eight: Research the Image

Depending on the scope of your project, you may want to engage in research on your topic. In your research, you will consult books, journals, and websites. Because images appear in many contexts, your work may involve investigating business journals for articles on corporate image and advertising, researching art history books for biographical information on particular artists or schools of painting, consulting theater journals for articles on set design, or browsing online dictionaries for terms used in design. You may even consult interviews with the creator of the image to discover what he or she intended. Biographies also provide insight into the thought processes of the imagemakers.

As you conduct your research, you will want to ask questions about the purpose of the information in the source material. Does the author intend to provide historical data to help readers better understand the social and material conditions under which a particular work of art came into being? Does the author intend to provide background data on a photographer's life? Is there a theoretical perspective that is strongly evident in the work, such as feminism and psychoanalysis? Is the piece offering a value judgment on whether an image is good or bad?

> **Links**
>
> Consult your library's print or online holdings for the following indexes:
>
> *Art Full Text.* Refereed and popular articles on folk art, graphic arts, and art history.
>
> *Grove Dictionary of Art.* Encyclopedia entries on artistic periods, movements, and individual artists.
>
> *Oxford Reference Online.* Encyclopedia articles from several sources.

Depending on the purpose of the piece, the author may be creating **scholarship, critique,** or **theoretical criticism.** Each type of critical perspective begins, as you did, with a careful inventory of the evidence from the image itself; however, each will have a different result. The scholars will work from documents to position the image in its cultural, historical, and biographical milieu. The critics will offer a personal point of view that derives from their judgments as connoisseurs of many images. The theorists will use particular images to advance ideas about society, such as whether women are too often portrayed as the subjects of men's gazes. Each point of view is valuable for its contribution to knowledge about images; however, the perspectives are not interchangeable.

Step Nine: Prepare an Interpretation

After conducting an inventory of the image and gathering your facts, you will be able to make an informed interpretation of the image. Interpretation offers a thesis about the meaning of the image, but also can make an argument about the value of the image. Art critics generally emphasize the latter, making a judgment about whether a picture is worth study: Is the subject a good one? Is the technique well executed? Has the creator of the image been overlooked by generations of scholars and critics? Has the image been overvalued or undervalued? Art historians often use critical theory to frame their perspectives, drawing from social history, biography, psychoanalysis, and gender theories. Each of these theories of interpretation is complex and nuanced, the sum of numerous practitioners who developed and refined certain theories. A short list of the types of theories you may encounter in your secondary research appears below. You may also feel comfortable writing from within one of these perspectives yourself, as you conduct your analysis.

Criticism falls into two categories: **applied** and **theoretical**. Applied criticism is an interpretation that one writer (usually an art critic, historian, or teacher) has created about an image. The goal of applied criticism is to use biographical, historical, and theoretical works to illuminate an image. Theoretical criticism works with a particular school of interpretation, an idea from a prominent philosopher or critical theorist, or a critical term (such as intertextuality). The goal of theoretical criticism is to use an image or series of images to illuminate a problem, idea, or critical term. Although there are many different types of theoretical criticism, certain dominant approaches are evident in critical work today. A brief overview of these approaches includes the following six modes of interpretation. Consult the bibliography at the end of this book to pursue your own inquiry into the complexities and nuances of these schools of thought.

Structuralism   Structuralist critics tend to emphasize the binary differences that exist between signs. These oppositions, such as light/dark, sun/moon, and man/woman, demonstrate how the privileged term (usually *light, sun, man*) depends upon the marginalized term to create a synthesis, a whole, a unified meaning.

Deconstruction   While deconstruction and post-structuralism are not synonyms, they are part of the same critical impulse to read the ruptures and imbalances in the text (rather than the structuralist balance, pattern, and design). Post-structuralists acknowledge binary opposition, but interrogate and break the binary to demonstrate that one term is always privileged and another marginalized.

Feminism, Gender, and Queer Theories   Gender critics argue that notions of gender (what is "male" and "female") are constructed by social conditions such as education, religious dogma, and media representations. While we are born with a biologically defined anatomy, we learn what it means to be "feminine" or "masculine." Assertions that there is a basic nature that is embedded in men and women are essentialist, reducing identity to an irreversible set of characteristics. Critics thus examine the images, language, and societal assumptions (**ideology**) that construct identity.

Psychoanalysis   There are two schools of psychoanalytic theory: Freudian and Lacanian. Popular culture has disseminated the key ideas of Freud such as the tripartite division of the self into ego, superego, and id; dream analysis; the uncanny; penis envy; and the Oedipus Complex. Freudian psychoanalysis is generally used to examine the neuroses of the author or creator, rather than to examine the workings of the text. Freudian critics examine the manifest and latent content of the works, the *manifest* being the working of the conscious mind and the *latent* being the intrusions of the unconscious.

Lacanian psychoanalysis, on the other hand, is a psychology of reading that draws on the influences of deconstruction. Lacan developed his own language for reading texts, and many of his concepts apply to reading images, such as a theory of "the Other," which may be useful when considering images of human subjects. Like Freudians, Lacanian critics sense that the text is always suspended in a network of unconscious desires.

Marxism   Marxist criticism is actually the product of mid-twentieth-century thinkers who drew on the works of Karl Marx and Fredrick Engels, rather than a school of literary criticism that employs their writings as central texts. Marxist literary criticism is overtly political in nature. Texts and images are interpreted according to themes such as the class struggle. The social class of the author may also be considered in producing a Marxist analysis, since the access to class privilege (money, education, travel) may be unconsciously conveyed in the text.

Cultural Studies, New Historicism, and Cultural Poetics   One of the most prevalent modes of analysis, yet perhaps the most difficult to understand, is cultural criticism, which has emerged as a dominant force in literary, artistic, and historical criticism in the last half-century. Those who claim to be cultural critics work in an interdisciplinary field that may include literature, popular fiction, television, film, historical narrative, travel literature, art, and popular, classical, and folk music. Drawing from Marxism, the cultural critic examines the everyday aspects of cultural production (rather than the highly artistic products of the elite). Cultural critics look at the cultural context of a work drawn from popular or everyday culture. The choice of work may be a previously artistic text that has been televised or adapted to film, such as an adaptation of *Dracula,* or it may be authentically popular, such as a soap opera.

Re-Vision

In Chapter One, you were introduced to Emanuel Leutze's *Westward the Course of Empire Takes Its Way.* Using this painting as your subject image, you examined how scholars developed a method for examining the meaning of the image. You then were able to study the way that the image created a visual argument.

Use the image by Leutze for this RE-VISION assignment in which you write your own analysis of the painting.

This time through, develop your sense of visual discrimination, your ability to identify key elements of meaning. Beginning with the PREWRITING QUESTIONS, engage in a process of formal analysis, investigating the form and structure of the images. Examine the way that the artist uses **literal elements** of the image (**Elements of Design**) and **arrangement** (**Principles of Design**) of the individual elements of the image. Finally, after you have completed your analysis, reflect on what is gained or lost by focusing exclusively on the elements and principles of design rather than on the argument of the image.

PREWRITING QUESTIONS

- **Color and Value.** Is the original image in black and white? Is the image rich in many different colors? Are the colors predominantly warm, cool, or a combination of warm and cool tones? If the image is black and white, to what extent does it develop contrasts between light and dark areas (value)?

■ **Meaning.** Does the use of color or value contribute to the meaning of the objects in the image? Consider other color possibilities for the image; would different colors change the meaning?

■ **Line and Shape.** Trace the contour of the objects in the image. Are the lines curved or straight? Are there strong horizontal, vertical, or diagonal lines? Does the image feature persistent geometric shapes such as circles or squares?

■ **Texture.** Does the image make use of any simulated textures such as bricks, bark, or satin fabric? How is your response affected by the representation of the surface area or background?

■ **Space.** What is the relationship of one object to the whole of the image? Is the object surrounded by white space? Are objects closely spaced or far apart?

■ **Perspective.** Does your image have a sense of depth? What do you see in the foreground of the image? What is in the background? Do any of the objects in the image angle from foreground to background in order to draw attention to the horizon line or a vanishing point?

■ **Vantage Point.** Where are you situated as a viewer? Do you look down on the object? Do you have the illusion that you are looking up at it?

■ **Dominance.** Which objects in the image are emphasized as the most important? Do they announce their importance by their color, shape, texture, or other means?

■ **Balance and proportion.** In what ways are the objects arranged? Are larger objects placed in the foreground of the image, in keeping with objective proportions? Does an implied dividing line create mirrored halves of the image? Do elements of color, line, texture, or shape repeat themselves from one side of the image to the other?

■ **Pattern.** Are elements of the image (such as objects, textures, or gestures) repeated to form a pattern?

- **Contrast.** Are colors, light, and shadows used to present a comparison of objects within the image? What meaning is suggested by the dissimilarity?

In Focus: Images and Analysis

For this IN FOCUS writing and visual display essay assignment, search for images that can be used as examples of strong Elements of Design and Principles of Design. You will compose a written analysis of your own images. For example, look for advertisements, book covers, posters, billboards, a photo from a family album, or another type of printed, visual image that you can bring to the classroom and share with others. Begin your analysis with the PREWRITING QUESTIONS above.

You may want to go beyond the analysis of individual elements in the images to work with some of the other key concepts in this chapter. For example, you could study the symbolism of a posed, professional wedding photograph, the formal senior-year photograph in your high school yearbook, or your university's promotional materials. Next, you may choose to read against the grain and identify absences and overt biases in representation. For example, you might choose to write from a feminist position about the photography in wedding magazines.

On Display: Icons

The image on display for your analysis (opposite page) contains at least three overt symbols: the yellow traffic symbol for caution, the cow, and the UFO. Using Sassoon and Gaur's rubric for analyzing icons and symbols, create a written analysis of this image. What part of the sign makes "a mark on the world," as in a signature? What do the various symbols communicate visually? Do any aspects of the sign initiate a story? Does the sign project any kind of self-image onto the world? Does the sign offer information that needs to be quickly understood? The photograph is of a sign along Route 66 in Arizona, itself an iconic stretch of road. Does this knowledge of the context in which the image appears affect your analysis? The four circular dots along the lower right of the traffic sign are bullet holes; are they also symbolic?

3

Picturing Place

Natural and Vernacular Landscapes

One of the most common ways that Americans interact with the visual is through their experience of scenery and landscape. Whether traveling to the Grand Canyon, walking through a local park, planting flowers in a backyard garden, photographing the family against a shining lake on a camping trip, or taping a poster of a European castle to a dorm wall, people express an interest in natural and built environments.

Even everyday spaces make use of furnishings and décor to evoke positive responses in the people that use them. Restaurants use wall coverings, furniture, and music to create an ambiance that makes patrons feel good about eating there. Planet Hollywood and the Hard Rock Cafe use memorabilia from movies and popular music, such as shoes, shirts, and instruments. The Portillo's Hot Dog chain in Chicago uses Chicago history as its themed décor, and the Rainforest Cafe chain uses a rich forestlike interior almost as a stage or film set to place clients into an extraordinary scene as they dine. Retail stores like Laura Ashley and Outdoor World decorate their stores to encourage a seamless connection among décor, product display, and product use. Stores, restaurants, malls, museum displays, theaters, and other public spaces employ what Gunther Kress and Theo Van Leeuwen call **multimodality**, the capacity to simultaneously communicate with sound, image, and tactile sensation. Verbal language may be one of the modes of communication, but it is not the primary method of conveying an argument or meaning. As you consider how you interact with public spaces, extend your analysis beyond the visual to study sound, gesture, posture, and the sensory abilities of touch, smell, and even taste.

> **Key Point**
>
> Studying images may include assessing and understanding three-dimensional objects and spaces. This points writers in the direction of studying visual culture, rather than limiting themselves to two-dimensional visual artifacts.

In this chapter, you will explore two case studies about how the world around us evokes strong emotions and is persuasive: Yellowstone National Park as viewed by painter Thomas Moran and the establishment of Gettysburg National Military Park. Each of these spaces is physically present and the study of them requires an extension from visual cultural studies to lived experience. Often, when places are special to people because of their beauty, unique natural features, or history, individuals and groups work to preserve them. The U.S. National Park Service preserves distinctive scenery, battlefields, cemeteries, and significant historical buildings. The National Register of Historic Places is a listing of thousands of buildings "that are significant in American history, architecture, archeology, engineering, and culture." Local historical societies designate sites of interest to residents and attempt to preserve the character

> **Links**
>
> In addition to park information, the website of the National Park Service contains several online interpretive exhibits, including one of Thomas Moran's Yellowstone. Visit **http://www.nps.gov/**.
>
> The National Register of Historic Places is a division of the National Park Service. The organization maintains a database of historic buildings in the United States as well as ideas for creative projects and lesson plans for teachers. Visit **http://www.cr.nps.gov/nr/index.htm**.

of buildings through historical fittings such as windows and doors, paint colors, garden landscaping, and interior décor. Enthusiasts, historians, and travelers enjoy recording the **vernacular landscape**, an everyday style based on need and belief rather than established through tradition. Examples of the attractions of the vernacular landscape are the diners, go-cart tracks, rock shops, and miniature golf courses that populate old highways like Route 66.

Let us begin this exploration of picturing place with a look at the way the natural features of the American West inspired a nineteenth-century artist named Thomas Moran to create some exemplary landscape paintings.

Natural Landscapes: Yellowstone National Park

Often when we look at a photograph or a painting of a place, we look through its flat surface to the reality beyond. We treat the image as a window rather than as something created by an artist or amateur at a particular time for a specific reason. This faith in the **transparency** of the image often precludes us from thinking further about how it came into being or how it is being used (in books, on mantelpieces, in museums). Yet many times what we see—what has been photographed or painted— is the result of a complicated negotiation that allows some features to come to the fore and others to be ignored.

In the nineteenth century, landscape paintings became a popular mode of creative expression. As ubiquitous as the landscape painting is today, prior to the nineteenth century, the art establishment did not consider landscape to be a suitable genre for a painter to work in; the preferred modes were portraits and historical or religious subjects. When you look at a landscape today, then, consider that the creation resulted from an audience and a market for the effort. By the nineteenth century, changes in property ownership from royalty to independent landowners created a wealthy class of art patrons who sought to memorialize their wealth through depictions of their landholdings. People also began to travel more, as roads and carriages improved and railway systems expanded, allowing artists to travel to new sources of inspiration. After a time, engravings of distinctive scenic landmarks appeared in the popular press, enticing tourists to visit. Tourists were even taught correct ways to appreciate the natural surroundings;

guidebooks directed them to **picturesque** landscapes, those that had familiar elements of rustic irregularity such as gnarled trees with drooping foliage, dusky pathways, and lakes or mountains in the distance. Once upon these sites, the tourists often copied the scene into their sketchbooks. Picturesque European landscapes favored the ruin, such as the ruined abbey or castle; but America, lacking the great architectural history of Europe with its Parthenon, castles, and cathedrals, could instead boast an acceptable variety of scenic wonders: vast, clear lakes; dense forests; rocky peaks; and colorfully painted valleys. One of these great American wonders is Yellowstone Valley in today's Wyoming.

In the latter quarter of the nineteenth century, three exploration parties set forth to explore the Yellowstone region of Wyoming. These were the Folsom party (1869), the Washburn party (1870), and the Hayden party (1871). These were not the first expeditions to or explorations of the area that would be set aside as a national park. The landscape was long rumored to be "the place where Hell bubbled up," in the words of nineteenth-century trapper Jim Bridger. While we know Bridger's words are a somewhat fanciful description of the geysers and mud pools of the region, people of the time thought Bridger and his fellow trappers were hawking tall tales.

So prevalent was the attitude that the marvelous land of the hot springs was a fiction that the first exploration group of David E. Folsom, William Peterson, and Charles W. Cook doubted the significance of their own visual perception. An article based on their travels into the Yellowstone region was rejected by the *New York Tribune*, *Scribner's*, and *Harper's* magazines as being unreliable, but eventually saw publication in the *Western Monthly Magazine* in July 1870. In their account, Folsom and Cook exhibited a recurrent fear that their descriptions would be too florid and that they would

> **Key Point**
>
> Early written accounts of the Yellowstone region were disbelieved as being "too fantastic." It took images to persuade others that the site was real.

be treated as liars by the general public. They go so far as to note that "Language is entirely inadequate to convey a just conception of the awful grandeur and sublimity of this masterpiece of nature's handiwork."

With interest raised by the accounts of the Folsom group, General Henry D. Washburn organized a second expedition in August 1870. Washburn was the surveyor-general of Montana Territory and under his direction, Folsom and Cook supplied information for a new map of the Yellowstone region. Outfitted with this map and the diaries of Folsom and Cook, Washburn set forth to produce a more detailed and complete map of the region. Nathaniel P. Langford, who had served as collector of internal revenue for the Montana Territory until 1868, joined Washburn on the expedition. Together, the men enlisted seven or eight others (including bankers and civil servants), two packers, and two cooks, and the party was augmented by military escort of an officer and cavalrymen. This grand expedition was hailed with fanfare in the press and social circles of Montana. Just over a week into their journey, the company was able to make its first verification of the wondrous reports that had issued from trappers, traders, and miners. Lieutenant Gustavus C. Doane recorded in the official report:

A column of steam rising from the dense woods to the height of several hundred feet, became distinctly visible. We had all heard fabulous stories of this region and were somewhat skeptical as to appearances. At first, it was pronounced a fire in the woods, but presently some one noticed that the vapor rose in regular puffs, and as if expelled with a great force. Then conviction was forced upon us. It was indeed a great column of steam, puffing away on the lofty mountainside, escaping with a roaring sound, audible at a long distance even through the heavy forest.

> **Discuss**
>
> Compare this verbal description of Yellowstone with the images created by Thomas Moran or with more recent photographs. Which medium is a more persuasive picture of place?

Despite the greater numbers of eyewitnesses on the 1870 Washburn expedition, the public was still skeptical of the published descriptive verbal reports, fearing by this time that an elaborate and prolonged hoax was being foisted upon them. The Denver *Daily Rocky Mountain News* published excerpts from Washburn's record of the sight of the thermal geysers as "A Montana Romance" in October 1870, and the editors prefaced the excerpts with a cautionary note that "while it may interest and astonish the reader, will also draw somewhat on his powers of credulity." While the *New York Times* published the Washburn account in full, and lauded its unpretentious rhetoric, it nonetheless noted to readers that "this record reads like a fairy tale . . . so gilded with true romance."

Nathaniel P. Langford produced from this trip a lengthy manuscript, which he presented publicly as a lecture and prepared into an article for *Scribner's Monthly*, "The Wonders of the Yellowstone." His amateur sketches and verbal descriptions were turned into woodcut illustrations by a young painter named Thomas Moran. Without a first-hand knowledge of the terrain himself, Moran was charged with inventing the geologic formations described in Langford's prose. His attempt was admirable, but, as he knew even then, most likely fell far short of representing the real. Thus, Moran was inspired to travel westward to see with his own eyes the wonders of Yellowstone.

Around this time, two significant developments in the history of Yellowstone took place. First, Dr. Ferdinand V. Hayden, head of the Geological Survey of the Territories, was an audience member at one of Langford's lectures of Yellowstone. Second, Jay Cooke, president of the Northern Pacific Railroad, was desirous of expanding the railroad's business into the area. Hayden was subsequently assigned by Congress to complete an accurate map of the region, one that would include the source of the Yellowstone River, and that would give "attention to the geological, mineralogical, zoological, botanical, and agricultural resources of the country." He was ordered to take artists and photographers with him "for the illustration of your final reports." In the days before color photography, artists provided an added dimension to the documentation needed for a successful expedition. With the assistance of the railroads and military, who provided transportation, supplies, and escort when necessary, Hayden was able to equip a full party of explorers by summer 1871 that included two artists (Henry W. Elliot and Thomas Moran) and two photographers (William H. Jackson and George B. Dixon).

Moran joined the expedition at the request of railroad magnate Cooke, who was hoping to lure train travelers to the West with the aid of stunning—and accurate—visual imagery. Moran hoped to create material for a second *Scribner's* article on Yellowstone by Langford, as well as offer his images to the official report of Hayden's and to assist his patron Cooke. On his trip, he filled several sketchbooks with charcoal and watercolor drawings, notes, and field studies. Moran also kept a diary of his travels.

During the trip, Moran made friends with photographer William H. Jackson. The two artists shared ideas about the best ways to represent this strange western landscape. They realized that they had a complex assignment: they needed to provide geographic evidence to Congress; they had to artistically interpret the mood of the place in order to secure viewers' emotional attachment to the landscape; and they had to offer awe-inspiring images that would attract tourists to the region. These goals were not often in harmony with each other, for too many tourists, hotels, railway stations, and roads could destroy the very land that Congress was seeking to protect.

The photographer Jackson employed a variety of techniques to suit his purpose. He took photographs at times of day when the shadows traversed the deep crevasses, used different lenses to compress or expand the landscape and to play upon the viewer's sense of space, and altered the angle of the camera to change the position of the viewer in the scene.

With pencil and watercolor as his medium, Moran had the flexibility to alter the literal elements of the landscape. He could toy with perspective, shade lightly or heavily, and experiment with color. Intentionally dramatizing the scene through perspective manipulation, color, value, and use of space, Moran was able to create responses in viewers who trusted his images. He completed several watercolors while on the tour and later, when he returned to his studio in the east, he composed several large oil canvasses of the grand vistas, such as the famous and exuberant 1872 *Grand Canyon of the Yellowstone*, which once hung in the halls of Congress, but which

> **Discuss**
>
> How ethical is it of artists to use "artistic license" in creating an image? Moran was charged to create an accurate record of Yellowstone. Did he accomplish that if he felt free to change colors and perspective?

is now located in the Smithsonian American Art Museum. *The Grand Canyon of the Yellowstone* measures nearly seven feet high by twelve feet across, a size intended to convey the magnitude of the landscape itself. To look at the painting is to look at something larger than the average man or woman. Immensity and grandeur are conveyed physically on paint and canvas.

By December 1871, with the assistance of an accurate map and supporting photographic and artistic evidence, Congress voted to create Yellowstone National Park. On March 1, 1872, President Ulysses S. Grant signed the bill into law. Jackson commented that his photographs and Moran's watercolors "were the most important exhibits brought before the [Congressional] Committee" because they finally allowed the disbelievers to see the wonders of this strange and beautiful land. In these days of Expedia, Hotwire, digital modems, and cable TV, it is worth reiterating that many members of Congress had not seen Yellowstone in person or in pictures. There simply was no way to gain sight of the landscape other than an extensive journey. The importance of these early images was immense.

Thomas Moran, *The Grand Canyon of the Yellowstone, 1872*

Smithsonian American Art Museum,
Lent by the Department of the Interior Museum.

Moran adopted the middle name "Yellowstone" after the Hayden expedition. He made many more trips to the West, painting its "Grandest, Most Beautiful, or Wonderful" scenes and dedicating himself to his doctrine that "the business of a great painter should be the representation of great scenes in Nature."

Rereading Thomas Moran's *Grand Canyon of the Yellowstone*

In Chapter One, you looked at the relationship between text and images. Images are frequently construed to be a supplement to text; the image depends on written language to make it intelligible to an audience. In the case of Moran's Yellowstone sketches and paintings, however, the opposite was true: words were distrusted and the images were required to verify the words.

Using Moran's working method as your own, experiment with words and images to describe a place. With a partner, find an area that can be represented as a landscape and visit the area with a notebook and sketchpad or camera. The area might be an urban streetscape or a traditional, parklike natural area. Individually, describe the area in words, paying attention to sensory description, especially sight, sound, smell, and touch. Compare your written descriptions. Did you focus on the same features? How are your written descriptions different?

After completing the written exercise, draw or photograph the same scene and compare the images to the words. You will notice that words are able to capture details that the images cannot. On the other hand, the images may convey a significance that is unavailable to language.

You might also consider sharing your writing with the class and asking classmates to create a sketch from the written description you provide. This excerpt from inveterate nineteenth-century traveler and writer Isabella Bird's narrative *A Lady's Life in the Rocky Mountains* (1879) may help you get started. How would you draw the scene that Bird describes below? Would a camera be in a better position to help you re-create the image? Why or why not?

> At the foot of the precipice below us lay a lovely lake, wood embosomed, from or near which the bright St. Vrain and other streams take their rise. I thought how their clear cold waters, growing turbid in the affluent flats, would heat under the tropic sun, and eventually form part of that great ocean river which renders our far-off islands habitable by impinging on their shores. Snowy ranges, one behind the other, extended to the distant horizon, folding in their wintry embrace the beauties of Middle Park. Pike's Peak, more than one hundred miles off, lifted that vast but shapeless summit which is the landmark of

southern Colorado. There were snow patches, snow slashes, snow abysses, snow forlorn and soiled looking, snow pure and dazzling, snow glistening above the purple robe of pine worn by all the mountains; while away to the east, in limitless breadth, stretched the green-grey of the endless Plains.

Finally, consider why tourists today photograph the sites that they visit. What advantage does the camera provide the traveler that the notebook and sketchpad do not?

Vernacular Landscapes: Gettysburg National Military Park

Prevalent in American visual experience, although often overlooked as a significant site of visual engagement, is memorial space. Memorials take different shapes and forms, ranging from historical markers on buildings or along roadsides to obelisks such as the Washington Monument in Washington D.C., and to figures such as mounted horsemen, and decorative monuments in stone or granite. Even open spaces that can be toured by foot or by car—such as Little Bighorn in Montana—can be memorial space. Such memorial spaces share a significant value—they allow viewers access to the past, acting as a window onto previous actors and events at each particular scene.

Using the basic scheme that asks us to consider why images are produced and how they are consumed, this section focuses on the memorial markers at a significant American site of memory: the site of the Civil War battle at Gettysburg, Pennsylvania, that took place over 1–3 July 1863. The small town of Gettysburg was where Confederate forces under General Robert E. Lee met Union forces under General George Meade. Fighting extended over an area of farmland and orchards several miles wide, leaving an estimated fifty thousand men dead, wounded, or missing by the end of the three-day engagement. The Union emerged as strategically victorious in the conflict, which was meaningful because the battle was fought on Union soil. In November of 1863, President Abraham Lincoln visited the cemetery where the Union dead were buried and delivered a short address (now known as the Gettysburg Address) that consecrated the site as hallowed ground, sacred space because it held the blood of fallen soldiers. His exact words were, "[W]e can not dedicate—we can not consecrate—we can not hallow—this ground. The brave men, living and dead, who struggled here, have consecrated it, far above our poor power to add or detract."

Lincoln's address set in motion conflicting reactions to this site: the memorialization of fallen men through battlefield markers and the tourist industry's marketing of Gettysburg as a noteworthy site to visit. The first memorial was erected in 1879; however, the first tourists had arrived in 1863, even prior to Lincoln's visit to the site in November, and reunions of the soldiers who fought at the site began as early as 1870. Today, tourists see the granite memorials that northern and southern states erected upon the ground that is now owned and maintained by the National Park Service. They also express a complicated desire to imaginatively return to the past by visiting the site, and, due to the efforts of several preservation groups, work has been underway for some time to return the grounds to the way that they looked for three days in July 1863. The effort is called **historic integrity** and involves burying utility lines, returning forested areas to their nineteenth-century appearance and use, and refurbishing farmhouses and fencing. It is argued that these efforts to establish the **visual purity** of the site will also enable present-day visitors to see what the soldiers saw. Of course, they will see the terrain that the soldiers had before them, but not the casualties.

Questions about what visitors to the battlefield see, who controls what is visible, and what meanings are available to visitors are important to those who study the rhetoric of place. In the century and a half that has ensued since the battle, tourists have visited the site by carriage and car. Following World War II, there was a period of "patriotic tourism" that swept the nation. Today, travelers and tourists are more likely to be persuaded by **heritage tourism,** the desire to experience the past through **living history** displays, costumed reenactment, and the restoration of buildings and landscapes to their premodern appearance. Heritage tourism offers a historic stage set for visitors to re-vision the past as it looked—even smelled—one hundred or two hundred years ago. Perhaps the most famous living history site in America is Plimouth Plantation in Massachusetts, which re-creates life as it looked and felt for seventeenth-century European settlers.

Yet, Gettysburg makes an interesting case study because it is not a museum, but an actual city in which people live and work. In

Gettysburg, history, time, memory, and modern development collide. The Kentucky Fried Chicken restaurant sits opposite a section of the battlefield. Those very soldiers whose bodies consecrated the earth in 1863 may have lain upon the future foundations of the KFC. The modern George Pickett All You Can Eat Buffet is next door to the historically recognized headquarters of General Lee. Military historians, both professional and amateur, vie with the needs of the current townspeople to restore Gettysburg to its appearance (or perhaps it is better to use the plural and say "appearances") in July 1863. While visitors may hear a contemporary military band in costume and witness the sound of cannon and musket fire at a demonstration or reenactment, they cannot hear the actual sounds of anguish that pour from a battlefield. The restorative efforts will always be most complete at the visual level.

Writer at Work

In this excerpt from Sacred Ground: Americans and Their Battlefields, *historian Edward Tabor Linenthal examines the development of memorials at Gettysburg. He explains that what contemporary visitors see at the National Park Service site is the result of negotiation and regulation. As Linenthal points out, one problem with erecting memorials is deciding who will be commemorated. Early in the process of commemoration at Gettysburg, a controversy erupted over whether to allow Confederate memorials on the site of Union victory. Charges of "favoritism" erupted, which were actually charges of how the story should be told and remembered. Who would emerge as the protagonist and the victor? At a larger level, the NPS was faced with the question of what visitors should learn and remember when visiting the site of battle.*

Edward Tabor Linenthal is a professor in the history department of Indiana University. His many works on historic memorials have traced the negotiations that take place as individuals and groups seek to represent complex events visually. His publications include Preserving Memory: The Struggle to Create America's Holocaust Museum *(1997) and the* Unfinished Bombing: Oklahoma City in American Memory *(2001).*

Sacred Ground: Americans and Their Battlefields

Edward Tabor Linenthal

Between 1895 and 1905 the battlefield was marked in detail: narrative tablets were erected to denote positions of troops, cannon were accurately placed, roads and fences were built, and thousands of trees were planted.

Until 1878 monuments commemorating the Union dead were placed only in the cemetery: the Soldiers' National Monument, a marble urn dedicated to Minnesota veterans, and the famous statute of Maj. Gen. John Fulton Reynolds, who died instantly from a bullet to the head as he led his men against Confederate forces. As the GAR [Union army, the Grand Army of the Republic] grew stronger and military units that had participated in the battle were invited to erect memorials on the battlefield, a new era in monument activity began. In 1878 and 1879 Pennsylvania GAR posts erected memorials to Col. Strong Vincent and Col. Charles Taylor. The monument of the Second Massachusetts Regiment, dedicated in 1879, was the first regimental monument on the field and the first to honor living veterans in addition to serving the traditional funerary function. By the time of the twenty-fifth reunion in 1888 the landscape had been transformed by more than three hundred monuments.

From 1884 until 1894 monument dedications almost always took place during the anniversary of the battle. By the twenty-fifth anniversary many Northern states had passed (or were in the process of passing) bills authorizing state funds to erect monuments at Gettysburg. In 1887 the battlefield commission developed certain guidelines: that monuments had to be of granite or bronze and had to provide information about the unit—its position, strength, and casualties; that statues had to face enemy lines; and that careful attention had to be given to the monument's foundations and the natural setting, for the "pleasing effect of a beautiful monument may be entirely neutralized by untidy surroundings." On March 3, 1893, Congress declared that all tablets marking

Linenthal, Edward Tabor. *Sacred Ground*. Copyright © 1981, Illinois University Press.

lines at Gettysburg should carry a "brief historical legend, compiled without praise and without censure." Recent policy does not substantially deviate from these early statements. Today, the approximately thirteen hundred martial megaliths that seem to emerge naturally from the ground are an enduring statement of patriotic veneration—in Stephen Vincent Benét's words, "startling groups of monumental men."

Early monuments represented efforts by veterans to memorialize their own heroism and to honor the sacrifice of their martyred comrades. At dedication ceremonies speakers often assured those gathered that even though contemporary society might seem indifferent to the veterans' former role as saviors, the monuments would stand for all time, despite the corroding forces of commercialism, forgetfulness, or historical revisionism. Whether they were designed to honor regiments, individual common soldiers, or generals, these monuments of bronze and granite would remind future generations of the power of heroism and unchanging principles on the battlefield. During the dedication of the First Maine Infantry Monument on October 3, 1889, Bvt. Maj. Gen. Charles H. Smith, who had commanded that unit, assured listeners that future visitors to Gettysburg would rely on these monuments to tell the story of the battle. "These monuments, their emblems and legends that mournfully decorate this great battlefield . . . will become [future visitors'] interpreters and assistants," he said. According to Gettysburg hero Daniel E. Sickles, who spoke at the dedication of the Forty-Second New York Infantry Monument on September 24, 1891, these monuments also served as permanent reminders to the nation of the need for martial revitalization. He noted, "There is no better way to prepare for the next war than to show your appreciation of your defenders in the last war. No nation can long survive the decline of its martial strength. When it ceases to honor its soldiers, it will have none."

The ideology of reconciliation also fostered growing pressure to mark correctly the Confederate lines and dictated that Southern veterans be invited to raise their own monuments on the battlefield. Only two Confederate monuments—one of which stood near the Angle and honored Brig. Gen. Lewis Armistead—were erected prior to 1888.

By the middle of the 1890s there was widespread feeling, in the North at least, that the monumental landscape at Gettysburg should more fully tell the Confederate story.

In 1896, for example, the *Philadelphia Times* stated that no "sectional passions" could interfere with attempts to "tell the whole story of the matchless courage of American soldiers." For some, the entire story was necessary in order to appreciate fully the holy crusade of the Northern troops. The *Gettysburg Compiler* declared in 1903 that a fully monumented field would show that the "God of battles gave the victory for the preservation of the Union" and that the battle was evidence of "immortal Anglo-Saxon bravery."

On June 8, 1917, Virginia became the first former Confederate state to erect a monument at Gettysburg, dedicating the equestrian statue of Robert E. Lee looking over the field of the Pickett-Pettigrew charge from Seminary Ridge.

A dozen years passed before another former Confederate state—North Carolina—raised a monument at Gettysburg. Alabama followed suit in 1933. The remaining states of the Confederacy did not begin to place monuments on the battlefield until the 1960s: Georgia, in 1961; Florida and South Carolina, in 1963; Texas, in 1964; Arkansas, in 1966; Louisiana and Mississippi, in 1971; and Tennessee, in 1982.

Despite the growing popularity of the ideology of reconciliation, controversy attended the construction of Southern monuments at Gettysburg. During the planning for the Confederate Soldiers and Sailors Monument, dedicated on August 8, 1965, Frederick Tilberg, the Gettysburg park historian, objected to an inscription that characterized the Confederates as defenders of their country. He noted that the opposite was closer to the truth, namely, that "they came rather near to disrupting their country." In a similar vein, George F. Emery, the park superintendent, questioned the Mississippi Gettysburg Memorial Commission's use of the phrase "righteous cause" on the monument it intended to dedicate on June 11, 1971. Emery hoped that "a substitute could be found or perhaps [the phrase] could simply be eliminated," neither of which happened. For their part, some Southerners thought that the Confederate monuments, once erected, were not being treated with the same care as Union monuments. A 1965 visitor wrote to the National Park Service about conditions at the North Carolina monument: "Imagine our dismay and indignation upon finding the North Carolina section partly encircled by a dingy clothesline type rope, limply strung through lead pipes which were lopsidedly driven into the ground." This, the visitor thought, was a "desecration of the memory of our fighting ancestors" and an example of the South "being slapped around again."

A related issue was the positioning of monuments on the field. As part of its goal to safeguard the integrity of the monumental landscape, the GBMA [Gettysburg Battlefield Memorial Association] (and later the battlefield commissioners) successfully resisted attempts to place Confederate markers at the points of greatest penetration of Union lines (the stone marker where Brigadier General Armistead fell at the "high water mark" representing the only deviation from his policy). However, debates over spatial contamination were not confined to North versus South. In 1888, for example, the survivors of the Seventy-second Pennsylvania Infantry, which had plunged forward to help throw back the Pickett-Pettigrew charge, insisted that their monument be placed at the point where the unit had engaged Confederate forces. The GBMA wanted them to position the memorial twenty feet farther away from the Angle, since another Pennsylvania unit had also seen combat at that forward position. In the summer of 1888 members of the Seventy-second defied the GBMA, broke ground for a monument at their chosen spot at the Angle, and were arrested for trespassing. The case eventually made its way to the Pennsylvania Supreme Court, which on April 2, 1891, decided in favor of the veterans. At the dedication of the monument on July 4, 1891, Capt. William Kerr's address revealed the importance for survivors of proper location. After a dramatic description of the hand-to-hand fighting, Kerr declared: "To this place, this unknown spot, you have given name and fame. It is recorded in history 'The Bloody Angle at Gettysburg.'"

Southerners also engaged in internecine struggles over appropriate locations for their monuments. Shortly after the battle Southern newspapermen, led by the influential Peter Alexander, provided reports on the battle to the *Savannah Republican* and the *Mobile Register*. They lionized Pickett and his Virginia troops and minimized the contribution that soldiers from other states, notably North Carolina, made in the Pickett-Pettigrew charge. Such favoritism was not easily forgotten. On August 24, 1921, Walter C. Clark, chief justice of the North Carolina Supreme Court, gave a speech to the Confederate Veterans Association and noted that Pickett commanded only three Virginia brigades in his division.

There was, said Justice Clark, "no reason why the assault should have ever been styled 'Pickett's Charge.'" He emphasized that troops from North Carolina had advanced "80 yards further to the front," and while there was "glory enough for all, the North Carolinians beyond all question went farthest to the front at Gettysburg."

Like the squabbles between New England towns over where the first "true" battle of the American Revolution took place, the state rivalries over the scope and positioning of Gettysburg monumentation were passionate affairs and were taken seriously by those who sought to preserve appropriate patriotic memories for coming generations. The placement of a monument a few feet in front of or behind that of another state or another regiment conveyed, for those concerned, a message about the impact of that particular unit or state on formative events. In consequence, there was an ongoing struggle to attain bragging rights at Gettysburg—that is, a struggle to dominate ceremonial space and gain permanent symbolic hegemony through the strategic placement of monuments.

Commemorative activity, whether in the form of patriotic rhetoric at anniversary celebrations or monument building and dedication, reminded participants that the ground they were standing on had been transformed by the potency of battle. Consequently, it became crucial to preserve, protect, and restore the field at Gettysburg, to freeze the landscape in its 1863 form. When Congress established the Gettysburg National Military Park in 1895, it gave the battlefield commission authority to purchase land according to a map prepared by Daniel E. Sickles. However, it failed to provide federal boundary legislation. The Sickles Plan called for a maximum procurement of almost four thousand acres, but a broader interpretation of the plan gave the government the authority to purchase more than fifteen thousand acres. As modernity, in the form of housing developments and commercial properties, began encroaching on the park, preservationists lobbied to incorporate into the park portions of the battlefield that were becoming indistinguishable from the rapidly developing secular landscape. They argued that the establishment of appropriate boundaries would preserve endangered land, define points of contact between sacred and secular environments, regulate such contact, and serve to protect the environment from physical or aesthetic defilement.

In 1974 the National Park Service submitted to Congress a proposal for new park boundaries. Critics of the proposal felt that it left out crucial areas. The controversy came to a head in 1986 when the Gettysburg Battlefield Preservation Association (GBPA), a private, nonprofit organization, tried to donate to the NPS thirty acres of land on which fighting between Union and Confederate troops had taken place. Since the land was outside the park boundaries, and since there was no legislation authorizing the NPS to accept donations of private land, the offer had to be rejected. Largely as a result of this incident, in 1988 Congress requested that the NPS conduct yet another boundary study.

The size of the battlefield at Gettysburg has always been a source of tension between administrators of the park—first the War Department and then, since 1933, the National Park Service—and residents of the town. Because the battle raged over vast areas, including the town itself, residents have often felt threatened by the expanding boundaries of the park, just as battlefield preservationists have often felt threatened by the lack of local zoning regulations, the creeping tentacles of freeways, and the growth of new housing developments. The recommendations of the newest boundary study only served to increase some local residents' fears of living in an "island town" in a vast sea of commemorative space. In 1980 William F. Goodling, a Republican congressman from Pennsylvania, spoke for the prodevelopment forces, as well as for a secular interpretation of the battlefield, when he said that the government should not be obligated to buy "every piece of land where a Union or Confederate soldier stepped."

Another area of concern for preservationists has been the visual sanctity of the battlefield—in other words, the need for it to look historically accurate (an integral element in veneration). During the twenty-fifth anniversary trees were planted in Ziegler's Grove to restore its 1863 appearance. Similarly, in 1909 the battlefield commission declared that an important part of its task was "to preserve the landmarks and appearance of the field as it was during the war, and with this purpose in view trees have been replanted in positions where they existed at that time, [and] undergrowth has been cut out."

Restoration and preservation of the battle landscape has always been one of the chief concerns of the National Park Service. The 1937 master plan of the Gettysburg park superintendent, James R. McConaghie, noted that the primary purpose of the park was to "preserve an area of great historical value in such a manner as to *permit the visitor to visualize conditions of the day.*" The "Battlefield Area Restoration Policy," formulated that same year, outlined the manner in which the NPS would eliminate undesirable "modern encroachments," namely, anything that introduced a "jarring note" and hampered the visitor's ability to visualize the battle.

According to the interpretive canons of the National Park Service, such "grounded imagination" was necessary to fully "experience" the battle. Since the early years of its stewardship at Gettysburg, the NPS has provided descriptive commentary on the battle along with occasional remarks on its legacy (what it calls "interpretation"). Previously, aside from formal ceremonies on commemorative occasions, visitors had to rely on the oral traditions of veterans, some of whom joined a growing number of battlefield guides. Guidebooks, visitors centers, and various other modes of interpretation later sought to orient and properly immerse visitors in the sacred environment.

Rereading "Gettysburg"

Unlike other writers whose works were excerpted in this book, Linenthal does not spend time describing visual elements of the scene. Instead, in a method similar to Cronon's work with the two-dimensional painting by Leutze (Chapter One), he tells the story of the place by re-creating events using dates and the names of people and places. He rehearses particular parts of the Gettysburg story that are familiar (if not sacred) to the audience. These include:

The Angle. A site of intense fighting in the afternoon of the third day, July 3, 1863. Confederate troops under the direction of General George Pickett, General Isaac Trimble, and General James Pettigrew attacked Union forces behind the stone wall at the Angle in hand-to-hand combat.

The High-Water Mark. Rather than an actual place, this is a metaphor for the turning of the tide in the Civil War to favor the Union, when the Confederates were repulsed at the Angle and withdrew from Gettysburg.

Pickett-Pettigrew Charge. The infantry advance upon Union positions led by General George Pickett and General James Pettigrew on the third day of battle, July 3, 1863.

Seminary Ridge. The grounds of the Lutheran Theological Seminary in Gettysburg, Pennsylvania. At the close of battle on the first day, July 1, 1863, Confederate forces occupied the ridge.

Linenthal's object is to look beyond the physical appearance to reconstruct the political forces that created the place as it appears now. From this viewpoint, all places have stories to tell that are not apparent to visual perception alone. Today, this aspect of storytelling is called the **backstory**, the retelling of a myriad of individual tales. As Linenthal notes, memorials aid historical storytelling, acting as "interpreters and assistants."

Yet, like William Cronon's analysis of Leutze's "Westward the Course of Empire Takes Its Way," Linenthal's argument encourages us to consider the way that memorial spaces evoke ideas of nationalism, heroism, and patriotism. Memorials are ideological; moreover, beyond their physical appearance as objects, their placement in the landscape—in particular countries, states, and towns—is crucial to how they are interpreted.

> **Discuss**
>
> If you were to create a memorial that expressed American idealism or any aspect of national commemoration today, what would you dedicate the memorial to? Where would you place it? Would any national heroes like Daniel Boone be included? Who are today's heroes?

Re-Vision

Linenthal discusses the constructed monuments that dot the wide area in which the Battle of Gettysburg was fought. Yet, there are additional visual spaces that are significant to the events that took place in the area. Here are two images of Gettysburg that are visually significant. What do you know about these images? What can you say about the need to maintain them in a historically pure manner? Is the cannon "decoration," an artifact, an integral aspect of re-visioning the past, or a combination of the three—decoration, historical artifact, and storytelling?

Through primary reaction and research, write a description of how the images create a meaning of place and time.

High-Water Mark: The copse of trees, a focal point for the Pickett–Pettigrew charge on July 3, 1863.

Little Round Top, Gettysburg National Military Park.

Even casual visitors to historic places will recall standard features such as narrative plaques that identify significant dates, characters, and events at the site. Every city features some type of historically commemorative memorial, perhaps the familiar rider on horseback. As Linenthal points out, memorials act as "interpreters and assistants," telling the "legends" of the past. As you look upon local or national memorial sites, have you found this to be true of your own experience? Have you learned to see your area differently based on the memorial markers? Is there a historical danger that commemorative monuments will become "invisible" to daily life? What will be lost if that happens?

In Focus: Images and Analysis

For this IN FOCUS writing and visual display assignment, find your own pictures of places to analyze and create a written analysis of your chosen images. Your texts may include advertisements (car manufacturers frequently use wild and rugged landscape to advertise their vehicles), real estate notices, or posters or brochures from tourist agencies. You might also visit an art museum or contemporary art gallery to seek out formal landscape paintings or photographs. Consider why the particular landscape is preferred over others. What purpose does the forest, beach, mountain, or street scene serve in advancing the ideas of the marketer? What purpose did the artist have in selecting the scene to re-create through paint or photography? Use the PREWRITING QUESTIONS prior to writing a formal essay to assess the area you intend to analyze.

You might even consider visiting a built or natural landscape. Disneyland and Walt Disney World are obvious examples of places that have been consciously created to evoke strong and pleasant emotions. Many new retail spaces try to create experiences for visitors that transport them to exotic locations, a type of space different in feel and appearance from the daily home kitchen. Restaurants like the Rainforest Cafe, Hard Rock Cafe, and Planet Hollywood go beyond ordinary decoration to attempt to alter reality and provide diners with a script for an alternative life scenario. Some larger local museums sponsor living history weekends. Many towns have a Renaissance fair or Medieval banquet. With a different purpose (to educate rather than entertain), living history museums create a stage where the sensations of the past can be performed and re-created by workers and visitors. Costumed reenactors perform "authentic" tasks (churning butter, dying yarn, firing cannons) with props in spaces that are constructed to represent buildings as they appeared in the past.

For this assignment, study a re-created site by visiting or consulting websites and publications. Examine what the organization chooses to re-create and how the "experience" of the place is presented to visitors. (For example, the Jorvik Viking Centre in York, England, goes so far as to offer the smells of the tenth century.) What elements of visual display are you conscious of?

PREWRITING QUESTIONS

- **Prior Expectations.** Before you visited the place you selected to write about or before you began searching for pictures, did you have any preconceptions about what you might find? From where did you get those ideas about the place? Books? Television? Music?

- **Multimodality.** Create a list of all the ways that a place can be experienced, focusing especially on the senses of sight, sound, smell, and touch. If you are investigating a place, consider how an ordinary place such as a coffee shop, restaurant, or retail store can be transformed into an "experience" for the consumer through lighting, decoration, and music.

- **Purpose.** The purposes of most public spaces in our lives are easily identified: restaurants are there for entertainment, libraries for education, grocery stores for food and household supplies. Beyond these purposes, however, spaces persuade us to feel comfortable and to enjoy being within their boundaries. What are the elements of persuasion of your space? Does it use the past to create a mood? Does it use familiar, warm themes such as "home"? Why was it created? How does it make you feel?

- **Storytelling.** Look closely at the story, materials, text, and figures on memorials, historic markers, or historic objects. How do these elements combine to tell a story? How do the places or things reflect the hopes, dreams, and fears of a culture or an individual?

On Display: Monuments

Seek out one or more commemorative monuments in your city. In a written essay, describe the physical characteristics of the memorial itself (using the rubrics of the Elements and Principles of Design), and then expand your essay further by looking closely at the site in which the monument stands and the sight lines of the person or people being commemorated. If it is a figure, does the hero gaze to the sea or at the city? What is the significance of the gaze? What is the gender and race of the figure? Consider what is absent from this scene. Could a different type of statue represent this event? Explore your local historical society to learn more.

Take this project one step beyond observation to creation. Select a recent event that might be worthy of commemoration and engage in a process of design and memorialization. What event will you represent? The Iraq War of 2003, September 11, the Columbine High School shootings, and the *Columbia* space shuttle crash are events that Americans will remember. Will your memorial be a plaque? An obelisk? A group of figures? Why have you made certain choices and rejected others? Will people read your memorial and note what is absent from its representation? Are you consciously working to represent all perspectives or are there significant aspects of the story that you are choosing to eliminate?

If you do not have a memorial to consider, use the image below as a discussion starter.

John S. Conway, *The Victorious Charge*, 1898.
Milwaukee, Wisconsin.

4

Picturing People

Smile and Say "Cheese"

When the camera was invented in the early decades of the nineteenth century, its effect on the way that Americans live their daily lives could not have been foreseen. Whereas prior to the mid-nineteenth century, the painted portrait was the medium of remembrance of the European and American social elite, photographic portraiture became a way to record the images of loved ones of any social class. The production of smaller, inexpensive, handheld cameras that could be owned by anyone of any economic background changed the way that Americans celebrated, traveled, and marked the passages of their lives. Imagine today a birthday party without a camera to record blowing out the candles on a cake.

Initially, ordinary citizens worked with still photography, but as handheld movie cameras became lighter, cheaper, and easier to operate, home movies were created by millions. One of the most famous home movies of the twentieth century is Abraham Zapruder's film of John F. Kennedy's assassination on November 22, 1963, in Dallas, Texas. On a break with his fellow employees from his job at Jennifer Juniors to witness the president's visit to Dallas, Zapruder climbed to a concrete barrier in the park to get a better view for his film of the president's motorcade. Using color film in a Bell and Howell eight-millimeter camera, he was horrified, five minutes after starting his film, to have recorded the image of the president's final day. Immediately recognizing the film's significance, he sought out federal investigators at the scene. "I'm just sick," he told a reporter shortly afterward.

Zapruder's experience in 1963 was echoed thirty-eight years later, on September 11, 2001 when thousands of workers and tourists in New York City witnessed the attacks on the World Trade Center. Hundreds of handheld video cameras and digital and traditional still cameras were

> **Link**
> Photographs of the effects of September 11, 2001 by amateur and professional photographers can be viewed online at **hereisnewyork.org.**

used to spontaneously record the terror of the moment. Later these photographs were included in a photographic memorial titled *Here Is New York* at www.hereisnewyork.org.

Today, the Photo Marketing Association estimates that thirty-three million Americans own digital cameras and process their own images. The camera is a ubiquitous piece of equipment in American life.

This chapter invites you to consider the ways that people have been pictured in family snapshots, painted portraits, cartoons, and documentary photographs; how photographers and artists represent race and class; and the extent to which the representation of the human subject is complicated by the intervention of the creator's motives and biases. The images are drawn from leisure and work. On your own, you may also extend the ideas of this chapter to advertising to question who is represented—considering race, class, and gender—and how they are depicted. Although cameras, easels, and paint are media used by human beings to capture the world and the people around them, we should always consider the ways that human creativity **mediates**—or interprets—reality. Images are used to make arguments and express opinions and several of the images in this chapter were designed with a particular political effect in mind.

Begin by thinking about a photograph in your own collection or one in the albums of your family. You might bring your high school yearbook to a class session and discuss the images in it. Is it easy or difficult to learn about a photograph just by looking at it? Do you know the people in the photograph? Do visual cues such as clothing style, props, or setting tell you when and where the image was taken? Do the props tell you what the human subject was thinking or feeling? Special clothes, such as gowns and tuxedos, might suggest a wedding or a formal party. Do you need to do research, such as asking your family about who the people are in the photograph or where the image was taken? Is there a special story associated with this image? Your teacher may also ask you to consider how the image was shaped by historical and cultural contexts. For example, if you are from Minnesota and your family photo album contains many years' worth of images of Hawaiian beaches and the rides at Walt Disney World, it may suggest that your family valued and had adequate resources to take annual trips to desirable locations. It may also suggest that your mother or father needed to get away from winter snows. Your teacher may ask you to consider how locations such as Hawaii and Florida come to the attention of tourists as "desirable" locations.

> **Key Point**
>
> Photographs do not represent the world openly; they are a vision of the world through the creative process of the photographer. This creative process is called "mediation," which means that the image is a third of the triangle of relationships that also includes the subject (photographer) and the object ("reality" being photographed).

Snapshots of Family and Travel

In January 2002, a Londoner named Mark McCarthy took a trip to the United States. He stopped in Las Vegas and flew in a helicopter over the Grand Canyon. Arriving back in London, he dropped his one roll of slide film off at the local Tesco supermarket, which used Kodak processing to develop prints. Unfortunately for McCarthy, the film was lost. Kodak sent him a free roll of film as compensation, but McCarthy was dissatisfied. "I feel as if Tesco and Kodak are treating my lost pictures as if they're unimportant and it doesn't matter," he told the London *Daily Mail* in June 2003. He sued Tesco and Kodak for losing his photos and was eventually offered about $8,000 in an out-of-court settlement to cover a return trip to the United States—so he could retake his photos.

The case raises questions about why people take vacation photographs. In a 1965 essay titled "The Cerebral Snapshot," travel writer and novelist Paul Theroux argues that setting the camera aside is "good for the eyes" and the vocabulary:

> Once, when I was in Italy, I saw about three dozen doves spill out of the eaves of an old cathedral. It was lovely, the sort of thing that makes people say *if only I had a camera*! I didn't have a camera with me and have spent the past two-and-a-half years trying to find the words to express that sudden deluge of white doves. This is a good exercise—especially good because I still can't express it. When I'm able to express it I'll know I've made the grade as a writer.

> **Discuss**
> Which tells us more about a place, photography or language? What similarities of mediation do they share?

Curmudgeonly as Theroux's comment may be, privileging the word over the image, the ancient art of writing over the modern invention, the question is a good one. Why take a photograph when traveling? Photographs of the Grand Canyon and Las Vegas are ubiquitous, part of the stock photography of clip art files of computer programs and advertising companies. Images of the Las Vegas strip are readily available through an Internet search such as Google's image search feature. If we want to see what the features are of the Grand Canyon or Las Vegas, these images serve as well as (and sometimes better than) our snapshots. On pages 87 and 88, the clip art images (top) are paired with images from a family photo album (bottom). Are there any significant differences between the paired images? Are there any cues that one is a professional photo while the other is a family photo?

Photo: Stock XCHNG.

Photo: Stock XCHNG

If looking at the features of a place is all we need to do, any of these images seems to suffice to create the idea of place. Why sue the processors of the film, then? The answer seems to lie with personal memory. The stock images represent someone else's experience, a stranger's presence, a memory of someone other than the viewer. Without the human figure, the scene is abstract and depersonalized. McCarthy reacted to the loss of his photos in much the same way that we react when something is stolen from us. It is not the image, but the memory that is lost.

When we take photographs at special events, we are documenting our personal histories. The photo provides evidence that we were indeed at the site on a particular day. Anthropologist Clifford Geertz has called this the verification of "being there." For example, while there are many photographs of New York City, there is only one taken of this subject in December of 2002.

The snapshot documents the American family ritual of travel. In addition, it unconsciously proves critic Marianne Hirsch's assertion that middle-class American children understand how to pose for the family snapshot: face forward, arms at sides, and smile ("say cheese!"). From our own family albums and desktop frames, we recognize this type of photograph and know how to interpret it. There is undoubtedly a parent or older sibling holding

> **Key Point**
> Because of the ubiquity of the camera, Americans are well versed in posing for pictures.

the camera and taking the photograph. In time, we look back at these snapshots to see not what New York City looked like in December 2002, but how we looked when we visited New York City that winter. The image becomes evidence of fashion styles and personal appearance. The image also serves as a reminder of the story of that event and may evoke feelings of sadness or joy. Perhaps this image was taken just before the girl fell ill, or just before she saw her first Broadway theater performance. As you look through your own photographs, ask yourselves these questions:

Who is present?

Who is absent?

How does the photo represent your life?

Is that representation accurate?

What power relationships does the photo reveal or obscure?

What key events—personal, emotional, social, economic—link up to the period represented in the photograph?

What scenarios are possible subject matter for your family's photo album?

What remains invisible in family archives?

In what ways does the photo prompt you to reconsider your self-history?

What social and cultural values and ideas shape the family's visual representation of itself?

Portraiture

A portrait is a picture of a person. Not all pictures of people are portraits, however. A portrait needs to be specially posed. Normally, someone with a special talent in photography or painting is hired to create the portrait. When you were in grade school and high school, you likely had your picture taken every year in the fall. During your senior year, you probably sat for a special portrait package and chose an image that was then published in the school yearbook. These special senior-year photos usually feature enhanced backgrounds. Some studios set up scenes with birch branches, ladders, or elegant chairs; many photographers take the image outdoors, perhaps with a dog, horse, car, or boat, or take it on the school's athletic field. Using props and clothing to show aspects of your personality in your senior-year photograph is part of a long tradition of portraiture. Before photography, painters were hired, usually by wealthy patrons, to create images of individuals and families. Some famous portraits that you may be familiar with are Gilbert Stuart's portrait of George Washington (1796) that now adorns the dollar bill; John Singleton Copley's portrait of Paul Revere (1768); and the mother-and-daughter paintings of Mary Cassatt. Compare these formal, painted portraits to your senior-year photographs. What do you notice that is similar?

> **Freewrite**
>
> Take a closer look at a yearbook from high school; it can be yours, a friend's, a family member's, or one in archives. Inventory the types of poses, clothing, and "props" that are used by the photographers to convey meaning. What do you learn about the people in the photos?

On a trip to an art museum, you may have passed by early American portraiture from the early eighteenth century. Typically, visitors to museums do not stop to study the early American portraits because the images are dark, flat, and simple. The individuality of the sitters' expressions seems to elude us. This is because the painters were self-taught; they are called **limners,** a word that means "to describe." Limners did not study perspective or anatomical drawing at art academies. They usually traveled from town to town, painting images of wealthy merchants and landowners. They frequently left their paintings unsigned. How might you begin to analyze these portraits? What are they telling us? Why would the person who is the subject of the portrait choose to be memorialized in paint?

One cue to the analysis of portrait is the prop. Just as your trumpet or tennis racket may serve to identify you as a musician or an athlete, the inclusion of a silver cup, a pen and paper, or a musical instrument is a cue to the attributes of that person. Portraits of a sitter on horseback indicate authority. (We are familiar with monuments and portraits of military leaders and royalty on horseback.) Portraits of men or women with their dogs often indicate favorable qualities such as faithfulness and loyalty. Similarly, the type of dog gives a cue to the person. A bulldog indicates strength; a cocker spaniel indicates domesticity. The props indicate what the sitter valued in his or her own life, but also what was valued in the time. If it was important to demonstrate literacy, the sitter was featured with pens and paper.

A second cue is the clothing that the person wears. The style of clothing may be formal and in dark colors. Is the sitter wearing a hat or is he or she bareheaded? Is the hairstyle tightly wound, disheveled, or free? What are the colors of the person's clothes? Black clothing traditionally represents scholarliness or seriousness and is often found in portraits of clergymen and judges. A young woman, however, might have chosen to be painted in pink, yellow, or pale blue, indicating delicacy and femininity. If a woman is the subject of the painting, how much of her skin is showing? If she is buttoned to her neck and wearing long sleeves, her portrait might be demonstrating her piety. In looking at your family photos or those in your yearbook, examine the color, fabric, and style of the clothing people wear. Are there clues to each person's beliefs, attitudes, interests, or personality?

A third cue to interpreting the picture is the gesture and gaze of the person in the portrait. Obviously, if the person is smiling, he or she is

Links

Gilbert Stuart's portrait of George Washington is in the National Gallery of Art, Washington D.C., **www.nga.gov.**

John Singleton Copley's portrait of Paul Revere is hung at the Museum of Fine Art, Boston, **www.mfa.org.** The Museum of Fine Art, Boston, also features a significant collection of Mary Cassatt's images to view online.

probably indicating a generous personality. Is the person sitting stiffly or leaning toward the viewer? Is the person in profile, like the woman in black painted by James Abbott McNeill Whistler in 1871, the painting now known as *Whistler's Mother*? Sometimes the subject points to something, perhaps out a window or behind a curtain. In George Gower's *Armada Portrait of Queen Elizabeth I* (1588–89), the defeat of the Spanish fleet that intended to invade England is shown through windows behind the queen. This portrait served to remind Elizabeth's subjects of her power. In her own words, drawn from her speech to the troops at Tilbury (1588), she might "have the body of a weak, feeble woman," but she was fortunate to have also "the heart and stomach of a King" and would defend her country to the death.

> **Links**
>
> *Whistler's Mother* may be viewed online at **www.ibiblio.org.**
>
> George Gower's *Armada Portrait of Queen Elizabeth I* can be accessed at **www.npg.org.uk.**

In the late eighteenth century, as painters began to broaden their subjects and increase their professional acumen, they combined landscape and portraiture into illustrative scenes. As author John Barrell demonstrates in the following excerpt, English painters were anxious to create a new national style of painting and turned to the countryside and its peasant inhabitants for inspiration. George Stubbs's painting *Haymakers* (1785) is one of several notable rustic scenes that Barrell includes in his analysis of the visual culture of the eighteenth century. He argues that paintings reveal a concern with the relationships of the rich and poor. Particularly, the paintings became a prescription for how field workers should act. Owners and employers expected the poor to be grateful for the opportunity to work, and thus work was depicted in imagery as healthy and morally uplifting. Stubbs's workers are, in Barrell's words, "strikingly tidy." Their clothing is spotless, well fitted, and fresh; there are no patches, no tears, no dirt. Noting the fashionable hats worn at an appropriately jaunty angle—as opposed to a cloth cap or a straw hat—Barrell wonders as well if the women are "dressed above their station," but questions also our desires to see the poor dressed in an appropriately impoverished style. As viewers of paintings whose subjects are farm laborers, on what do we base our judgments about the poor?

How should the poor be dressed? How should their labors be portrayed? Finally, Barrell asks viewers to consider whether these laborers are actually "the poor." The entire group is posed in a harmoniously choreographed line in attitudes that appear staged by models at the Royal Academy of Arts in London. It may be, he suggests, that painters such as Stubbs, whose works were purchased by the wealthy for display in their homes, had to present the workers in such a way as to be acceptable for framing and hanging in the homes of the rich.

George Stubbs (1724–1806) *Haymakers.*

1785, Tate Gallery London/Art Resource, NY.

Writer at Work

John Barrell is a professor in the Centre for Eighteenth-Century Studies at the University of York in England. His research examines the connections between painting and language, social politics, and law. In this excerpt from The Dark Side of the Landscape, *Barrell argues that we can understand painting better by positioning it next to the literature that was popular at the same time. Imaginative (aesthetic) works such as paintings and literature reveal the attitudes, values, and beliefs (ideology) of a culture. The title of his book comes from a review that appeared in the English periodical* The Gentleman's Magazine *in 1783. As Barrell explains, the phrase refers to a general principle of landscape painting that the rich and their property must be illuminated, while the peasant poor should be left in "the dark side of the landscape."*

The Dark Side of the Landscape

John Barrell

If we can be sure of anything about the eighteenth century, it is that English society at the time was minutely stratified and subdivided, and there is no level at which a line can be drawn around the social pyramid, marking off the "rich" from the "poor," or the consumers of Britain's wealth from its producers. Thus the tenant-farmer—an occupation in itself too capacious to be generalised about with any confidence—may well feel himself to be a producer in relation to his landlord, and poor in comparison with him, while to his labourers he will often appear as the rich consumer of the fruits of their labour; and similar conventions of authority and deference which govern the relations of landlord and tenant will govern those of tenant and labourer. There are difficulties, too, in thinking of the "labourers" as composing a homogeneous and recognisable class—for, as we shall see, many of them earned their living in a variety of ways, of which working in the fields of other men was only one, and there must have been significant differences in income among those who did, or did sometimes, thus hire out their labour. There is not one line but many, drawn by those in every station immediately above or below the position they feel themselves to occupy.

That is likely to be true, of course, in any developed or developing society; but what has often been denied about English society in the eighteenth century is that its members exhibit any consciousness of class at all, and it is asserted instead that in a society so stratified the lines are drawn not by classes but by individuals, aware of relations of difference between themselves and others above or below them on the pyramid, but not of relations of similarity with those at the same level—for the levels are too many, the occupations too mixed and various, to allow generalisations in terms of class to be made by those alive then, or by us now. This is not the place to discuss the issue in detail; but an acquaintance with eighteenth-century writing, whether with the imaginative literature or with the literature concerned more directly with the discussion of social problems, will reveal that the "poor" were indeed coming to be thought of as a class, as the distant generalised objects of fear and benevolence; and the widespread and continued necessity of keeping the labouring poor alive by supplementing their wages with public or private charity made the line dividing the poor from the rest of society brilliantly if misleadingly clear. And not to the politely literate only, but to the poor themselves, whose resentment of the erosion of their customary rights, of their own need—which appears to them often as the consequence of that erosion—for charity even when they were in full employment, and of the postures of cheerfulness, submission and gratitude they had to take up to receive it, was an important factor in creating a consciousness of solidarity among those who did, or did not quite, qualify for relief, and of difference from those who provided it, which must be understood as class-consciousness: us the poor, them the rich. It is this consciousness, on the part of the polite and vulgar alike, that I am appealing to when I appear to ignore the complexities of the society of the period, and refer so insistently to the "rich" and the "poor."

That in the context of my argument the term "rich" needs no further differentiation, I hope to show later in this introduction. Why in the eighteenth century the poor came to take on the status of an undifferentiated class, whose need for charity was their most distinguishing characteristic, is a problem that will not be resolved in this book; for it is by no means clear whether the poorest members of rural society did become significantly worse off between 1700 and 1800, or whether the greater awareness of the poor as a class that we observe among the rich in the last quarter of the century is in fact an awareness of the greater threat they posed to the stability of England, by reason of their increasing literacy and their own developing class-consciousness. There are good reasons for believing that the condition of the rural poor did indeed get worse. The long process of transforming the "paternalist," and what has been called the "moral" economy of English agriculture, into a capitalist economy resulted, as it was partly intended to do, in the reduction of the poorer members of rural society to the condition of a landless proletariat. At various times in different places, by different forces operating gradually or suddenly, the process enveloped many of the smallest freeholders and copyholders, and the miscellaneous individuals who had managed to put together a living by what they could earn as hired labourers and in some cases as the practitioners of crafts and trades, and by what they could make or find by exploiting the customary rights which, insignificant as they apparently often were, provided some sort of a cushion against the seasonal variability of agricultural employment, and some valuable sense of independence.

The enclosure of wastes and open fields, and the consequent extinction of common rights, was one method by which this proletariat was created, and we should not overlook the evidence that one motive for enclosure was, precisely, to make the labouring poor more dependent on their employers, and so more tractable to their discipline. But in fact, whether or not the rural poor did generally become poorer in the course of the century, it seems likely that their material condition was as desperate in parishes where rights of common had not been extinguished as where they had. The steep rise in population, the decline of the outworker system in the face of the greater mechanisation of the textile trades, and the system of parochial settlement, meant that in many parishes there were more labourers than could be employed, who became wholly or partly dependent on public and private charity.

It remains, in any case, by no means clear that the material condition of the poor was appreciably worse by the end of the century—the evidence is neither adequate nor, drawn as it is from so many different regions, susceptible of generalisation. It does seem clear that many of them had lost much of whatever degree of independence thay had formerly enjoyed, and this contributed to the creation of that working-class-consciousness that [. . .] was feared and resisted by the rich; but this loss of independence may not have led to an actual reduction in their material standard of living. That it was *evident* by the later decades of the century that rural labourers were in many regions unable to earn enough by their labour to support their families may equally plausibly be explained by what I have called a new awareness of the poor on the part of the rich, and I shall return to this point in my next section.

Whichever explanation we prefer, the continuing transformation of the agricultural economy remains the context in which the condition of the poor, and the art of rural life, must be discussed. The customary rights of the "moral" economy were not easily surrendered, nor the increasing emphasis on labour-discipline easily accepted, and in the works of [E.P.] Thompson there is much evidence of social conflict in the countryside in the period covered by this book. This conflict should not be interpreted as a matter of local and casual lapses from an overall stability, inasmuch as it almost invariably takes the form of resistance to specific changes in the economic and social order—of attempts, mainly on the part of the poorer members of society, joined sometimes by the better-off when their interests were threatened by the largest landowners, to preserve the customs of the old economy against the encroachments of the new. "The Plebeian culture," as Thompson has written, "is rebellious, but rebellious in the defence of custom". And yet this conflict is largely ignored by the poetry of rural life until the last decades of the century, and it never breaks the surface of the painting of rural life, except, as I shall argue, in a number of paintings by George Morland. For the most part the art of rural life offers us the image of a stable, unified, almost egalitarian society; so that my concern in this book is to suggest that it is possible to look beneath the surface of the painting, and to discover there evidence of the very conflict it seems to deny. The painting, then, offers us a mythical unity and—in its increasing concern to present an apparently more and more actualised image of rural life—attempts to pass itself off as an image of the actual unity of an English countryside innocent of division. But by examining the process by which that illusion is achieved—by studying the imagery of the paintings, the constraints upon it, and upon its organisation in the picturespace—we may come to see that unity as artifice, as something made out of the actuality of division.

It goes without saying that the paintings I discuss were produced for those who by this account, and at least from the perspective of the poor, were rich; and the "constraints" I have referred to were the constraints which governed how the labouring, the vagrant, and the mendicant poor could be portrayed so as to be an acceptable part of the *décor* of the drawing rooms of the polite, when in their own persons they would have been unlikely to gain admission even to the kitchens. These constraints still operate in subtle ways today, as I shall try to show in a brief discussion of Stubbs later in this introduction; so that when in the essays that follow I refer to "our" response to a picture, or to what "we" demand to see in the image of the eighteenth-century poor, it is not to be thought that I am confusing the amateurs of art today with the connoisseurs of the period covered by this book, but rather that we should ask ourselves whether we do not still, in the ways we admire [Thomas] Gainsborough, [George] Stubbs, and [John] Constable, identify with the interests of their customers and against the poor they portray. I am not suggesting that we should do anything else, merely that we should ask what it is that we do; to identify with the exhausted and underfed labourers is impossible for us, and would be insulting if it were not.

Realism, actuality, involves, reasonably enough, a need to portray the figures in landscape at work, and not idle as the shepherds of Arcadia were known to have been; so that in his ironic "Proeme" to *The Shepherd's Week*, [John] Gay proudly asserts:

Thou wilt not find my shepherdesses idly piping on oaten reeds, but milking the kine, tying up the sheaves, or if the hogs are astray driving them to their styes.

This insistence on a workaday actuality becomes indistinguishable from a demand that rustics *must* be shown as industrious, so that we have no way of telling a "straightforward" image of the poor at work from a prescriptive image of them as they should be, working. In the essay on Gainsborough we shall find enough evidence to suggest that in the middle of the eighteenth century an image of men at work was more than a neutrally "descriptive" one, but there is no clear evidence that at this time the demand for such images was a consciously *moral* demand. There was, indeed, little pressure on writers and artists to acknowledge the prescriptive aspect of a descriptive representation of work until, in the last decades of the century, the threat which the workers themselves might represent as an undisciplined, collective force was also recognised, as writers and artists in whom we may detect an overt or implicit radicalism appropriated the pastoral ideal, of a life of light labour, as a radical ideology, in the face of an increasing demand on the part of employers and moralists that the poor submit to labour as to a moral discipline.

As the rustic figures become less and less the shepherds of French or Italian Pastoral, they become more and more ragged, but remain inexplicably cheerful. The effort is always to claim that the rural poor are as contented, the rural society as harmonious, as it is possible to claim them to be, in the face of an increasing awareness that all was not as well as it must have been in Arcadia. The jolly imagery of Merry England, which replaced the frankly artificial imagery of classical Pastoral, was in turn replaced when it had to be by the image of a cheerful, sober, domestic peasantry, more industrious than before; this gave way in turn to a picturesque image of the poor, whereby their raggedness became of aesthetic interest, and they became the objects of our pity; and when that image would serve no longer, it was in turn replaced by a romantic image of harmony with nature whereby the labourers were merged as far as possible with their surroundings, too far away from us for the questions about how contented or how ragged they were to arise.

There were a number of unwritten but binding rules which governed the terms on which the poor could appear in landscapes at all, which for the most part were recognised only when they were broken. If these rules were not consciously obeyed by the painters, that is because, although they existed to protect the sensibilities of the polite, for a long time they operated in the paintings as aesthetic, not social constraints: what sort of figures of the poor look right in a landscape, and where do they look right, in relation to the organisation of the picture as a unity? In their responses to these questions, [painter] George Lambert, for example, and Gainsborough, and Constable, all reveal attitudes not to the poor alone but to the society as a whole, which may be their own, or their customers', or both; and in this way their paintings come to express what they or their customers wish to believe was true about the rural poor and their relations with nature and with the rest of society.

We can get an idea of the terms on which an image of the poor would "look right" in landscape from this comment by James Barry, made in a lecture delivered probably in the 1780s:

> There is no department of art which might not become interesting in the hands of a man of sensibility. Who does not feel this in the landscapes of N. Poussin, sometimes verging to sublimity, and always engaging from their characteristic unity, graceful simplicity, or ethical associations. Allowing for a little unnecessary rags and vulgarity; who is not also delighted with the serenity and innocent simplicity of many of the scenes [. . .] the simple, laborious, honest, hinds; the lowing herds, smooth lakes, and cool extended shades; the snug, warm cot, sufficient and independent; the distant hamlet; and the free, unconfined association between all the parts of nature, must ever afford a grateful prospect to the mind.

For a landscape to be "interesting," then, in the hands of a "man of sensibility," the "hinds"—the word calls attention to the degree of pastoral artifice which will be necessary if the image is not to offend us—must be "simple, laborious, honest," their cottages "sufficient and independent"—which is to say that the cottages must not attract attention to the distresses of the actual poor.

References, *The Dark Side of the Landscape*

Arcadia. An idealized concept of country living in which the rustic, simple life is presumed to be innocent and healthy. In Arcadia, the shepherds are noble and the maidens are proud.

Constable, John. 1776–1837. English landscape painter.

Gainsborough, Thomas. 1727–1788. English landscape painter.

Morland, George. 1763–1804. English landscape painter.

Pastoral. A work that depicts idealized rustic life.

Poussin, Nicolas. 1594–1665. French history painter.

Rereading *The Dark Side of the Landscape*

Barrell's analysis focuses less on the compositional Elements and Principles of Design outlined in Chapter Two than on social history. Rather than emphasize what the paintings depict, much of his analysis describes what the paintings deny: social tension between the classes, the threat to England from Napoleon and France, and the documentary portrayal of the lives of the working class. Whereas William Cronon's analysis of Leutze's painting *Westward the Course of Empire Takes Its Way* opens with a narration that animates the events and action of the painting, Barrell opens his analysis with history. He indicates that the painting is just one instance of a larger eighteenth- and nineteenth-century attitude toward the rural poor and the working class. In addition, rather than focusing on one painting as an instance of historical consciousness (as Cronon does in "Telling Tales on Canvas"), Barrell compares the work of several contemporaneous painters in order to show how groups of artists create attitudes and ways of seeing subjects, what we referred to earlier as **ideology**. It is evident from the focus of his writing that Barrell is concerned with the depiction of the worker in fine art. He hints that, although there was a degree of social unrest in the eighteenth century and that in

> **Key Point**
>
> John Barrell's Three-Point Sequence of Analysis
>
> 1. Historical context of production
> 2. Comparison to other works and painters from the same time
> 3. Formal elements

that time of the American and French Revolutions some feared that the lower classes would rise up forcibly against the landowners, the landscape paintings of the time erased any political questions in order to portray the countryside as a peaceful, harmonious place. Also at work in creating a particular kind of social climate, the Napoleonic wars (1793–1815) fostered a desire for English painting and poetry to be more patriotic, to depict English scenes realistically and accurately in order to document what was truly English. Prior to the time of Gainsborough and Stubbs, landscape painting was not only indebted to the Italian and French schools of landscape painting, but it also drew heavily on the dominant imaginative concepts of Arcadia and the pastoral.

Some of the key questions for examining portraiture and home photography can be asked of these paintings of the rural working life. Barrell's work asks us to consider issues of representation:

- Who is present in the image and how are those people depicted?
- How are relationships of power signified by the painter and the subject?
- What props are used to signify class, status, occupation, and gender?
- How does body position indicate values such as idleness or industriousness?
- In what way does clothing color or design reveal attitudes toward the subjects of the image?
- Are the gestures of the subjects significant?

The Politics of Race and Imagery

In the nineteenth century, illustrated newspapers and magazines became a common feature of the reading public's life. Prior to that time, illustrated texts were not typically mass-produced or distributed, but were reserved for specially illustrated volumes owned by people of means. Illustrations were often created after the event, when an artist was sent to the scene to re-create the incident from observation and eye-witness accounts. As we saw in the previous chapter, Thomas Moran created his first images of Yellowstone from verbal descriptions provided to him by an early explorer. News images in the nineteenth-century press might take the form of engravings worked from photographs made at the scene. Or the images might be a composite of impressions taken over time to give the spirit of the place and significant people. American painters Winslow Homer and Frederic Remington began their careers as reporter-illustrators for *Harper's Magazine*.

The illustrated news gazettes also featured political cartoons, a durable form of art that we still see today (and one that Bud Pisarek employs in his "Above All" cartoon strip featured in Chapter One). In the nineteenth century, in order to convey the personality characteristics of the subjects of the illustrations, many artists relied on a form of visual shorthand called "physiognomy"—the art of judging human character from facial features. Beginning in the eighteenth century, the study of human facial appearance took shape under the formal names *phrenology, craniology,* and *organology*. In general, proponents of the study of physiognomy claimed that the shape of the skull and nose, the set of the eyes, and the slope of the forehead provided a reasonably accurate indication of the mental capacity and personality of the subject. A staple of phrenology was the correspondence of facial characteristics to animal appearance. A sloping brow, for example, might be said to resemble a frog and thus indicate subnormal intelligence and a brutish personality. (Of course, what was considered "normal" was usually the intelligence and the personal features of the person doing the measurements.) Editorial cartoons created in response to the American abolitionist movement employed racial typing to persuade the public that the slaves were incapable of living independent lives and needed the structure of the plantation system.

> **Key Point**
> In the nineteenth century, the study of human features, called "physiognomy," influenced political drawing, caricature, and literature.

Cartoonists such as the British illustrator John Tenniel, familiar to many from his drawings for Lewis Carroll's *Alice in Wonderland*, used physiognomy to depict various "races" with whom the British had interactions in the nineteenth century. Because Britain's policies of empire had expanded its territories the world over, the number of non-Anglo-Saxon people with whom they had contact was considerable. The drawings alone are striking, for they illustrate without any textual explanation the derogatory, demeaning, and brutal attitudes toward various "Others." A catalogue of these nineteenth-century images reveals that, among other British subjects, the Irish, near neighbors, are depicted as monkeys, apes, pigs, cats, and an assortment of animal-human hybrids. The British, meanwhile, are represented by the ubiquitous and upstanding John Bull or a handsome lion, both indicating stalwart strength and integrity. Two illustrations by Tenniel blend the study of physiognomy with the anxiety caused by Mary Shelley's popular novel *Frankenstein* (1816). Frankenstein's creation, a revivified human, came to stand metaphorically for an aggressive—yet dependent—relationship between one country and another, the perfect construct for an imperial culture. Just as the creation desires the affection of his master, Victor Frankenstein, Ireland is constructed by the press to need the governmental care of the

British Parliament. The British, however, can only spurn what they characterize as the crude nature of the country, just as Frankenstein spurns his misshapen creation.

In Tenniel's "The Brummagem [Birmingham] Frankenstein" published in *Punch* in 1866, there are two figures. One is three times larger than the other. This giant wears a laborer's stocking cap, open shirt with sleeves rolled past the elbows, and unfastened hob-nailed boots. His arms rest on his knees in a mildly aggressive posture. He is stubble-faced and smudged by dirt. His right hand appears to be either dirty or chapped from rough work. Beneath him creeps a portly gentleman in a silk porkpie hat, frock coat, and polished shoes, perhaps John Bull.

A similar dichotomy between ruthless brute and gentleman is evident in "The Irish Frankenstein," reproduced below. Here, a looming, misshapen simian figure strides forward across the page. He clutches a knife that drips fresh blood. He wears a mask and cloak for a mysterious and murderous midnight escapade. The gentleman in the left corner of the page holds his hand forward as if in fear or warning.

THE IRISH FRANKENSTEIN.

"The baneful and blood-stained Monster * * * yet was it not my Master to the very extent that it was my Creature ? * * * Had I not breathed into it my own spirit?" * * * (*Extract from the Works of C. S. P-rn-ll, M.P.*)

John Tenniel, "The Irish Frankenstein."
Punch Magazine. Reprinted by permission of Punch Limited.

While these Irish images seem removed in time and space from our experience, their tradition of representation was not lost to history. It may surprise many that Theodor Seuss Geisel, the famous illustrator of the children's book *The Cat in the Hat*, worked as a cartoonist for a New York–based newspaper called *PM* from 1941 to 1943, the early years of America's involvement in World War II. Dr. Seuss employed the political cartoonist's—and propagandist's—tools in his war efforts, in order to both reflect and shape the American public's understanding and sentiments. Hitler was depicted with a puffed chest; his mouth was small and pinched under a dark moustache. The deluded French general Henri Phillipe Pétain was drawn as small, wrinkled, and bemused. The Japanese were slant-eyed and bucktoothed. The national consciousness supported such anti-Asian imagery and feeling. (After the attacks on Pearl Harbor, even *Life* magazine published an illustrated "news article" about how to tell the Japanese face from the Chinese face.)

> **Freewrite**
>
> Looking at cartoons and illustrations in today's newspapers, do you notice any dominant trends in representing ethnic groups, either from America or from other continents? What visual shorthand is used to depict the French, the British, the Afghan Taliban, or others? Do you see patterns of representation recurring in political cartooning? How do you think these images will look to viewers one hundred years from now?

Documentary Photographs

As illustrated journalism moved into the twentieth century, the camera became more portable; technology that enabled the electronic transmission of images across continents was developed; printing presses improved; and news items were increasingly illustrated with photographs. It wasn't until mid-century, however, that photojournalists created their own professional organization, the National Press Photographers Association, in 1946. Today, of course, newspapers are liberally illustrated with news photography; the front pages of most sections feature three to four photographs of varying sizes and subjects. As a journaling exercise, open up a copy of today's newspaper and count, list, and describe the images on the front page. Are these images portraits of people? Do they record events? Are the subjects

Links

A collection of Pulitzer Prize–winning photographs from 1945 to the present is online at the Newseum, **www.newseum.org/pulitzer/.**

well-known public figures? Is the mood of the photographs upbeat or serious?

In this section we consider the extent to which the representation of the human subject in documentary photography is complicated by the awareness of the presence of the photographer. The imagemaker is absent from the frame, but his or her presence is always sensed. It is only an illusion that we are seeing directly into the scene. Again, the subject is mediated.

Photographer Kevin Carter arrived in the African village of Ayod in the Sudan in February 1993. The country had been involved in civil war since 1956, and the ensuing thirty-seven years of strife had left villagers starving, diseased, displaced, injured, and dying. At Ayod, Carter photographed refugees arriving at a food station. There, he found a poor, weakened girl, stalked by a vulture. Carter made his photographs and chased the vulture off.

In March 1993, the *New York Times* published the photograph. It was soon distributed internationally and became an emblem of the suffering of the people in the Sudan. In 1994, Carter was awarded the Pulitzer Prize for feature photography. Almost as quickly, Carter's ethics were questioned by journalists. He was branded a vulture himself because, rather than intervening in the horror of the scene, he photographed it. The photograph carries no record that he attempted to help the girl. Devastated by the critiques and by the death of his friend, photographer Ken Oosterbroek who was caught in crossfire in South Africa, Carter committed suicide on 28 July 1994.

As you examine Carter's photograph, reproduced below, consider the critiques of Carter's image. Is it possible to represent the intensity of suffering in order to effect change without immediately physically intervening? Is this image a portrait? Is it a metaphor for suffering?

Photo: © Kevin Carter/Corbis Sygma

Re-Vision

As you learned in Chapter One, the creators of images employ a "syntax" or structure to be persuasive. Looking again at Carter's photograph, examine the elements that make it persuasive, drawing from John Barrell's criteria for examining the human figure in painting. Write an essay that addresses the following areas of analysis:

- Who is present in the image?
- What material elements (such as clothing, objects, setting) are present to signify class, status, or gender of the human subject?
- How does the body position or gestures of the subject carry meaning?
- How are relationships of power structured between photographer and subject?
- What is the significance of the camera's angle and point of view and the girl's inability or refusal to return the gaze?
- How does the compositional structure—the planar layout, foreground, and background—affect the interpretation of the image?

- Considering the proximity of Carter to the girl, how might the image have been different if the photographer had made the image from a point farther away from her?

In Focus: Images and Analysis

This IN FOCUS section is slightly different from those of previous chapters because you will create your own photonarrative and a self-reflective statement to accompany the essay. The two parts of this assignment are:

1. **Photo narrative.** You may use any type of camera to take a series of photographs that will eventually be displayed for your class. The arrangement of the photographs is critical to telling a story about the subject. How will your first image introduce your subject? How will the final image instill a sense of conclusion? While the photonarrative may include accompanying text, this is not necessary if the connections between your images are strong and invite viewer participation. One question that you have probably already asked yourself is what you would do with a camera, if you were asked to document a day in your life. What choices would you make about what should be included and excluded from your visual record? How would your images be intelligible to others? What visual cues would have to be present in order for the images to be understood? What literal elements of design would draw attention to your meaning and purpose? What would it mean for you to take photographs of daily life rather than special occasions? Would your images highlight problems or successes?

2. **Reflective statement.** Once you have made your photographs and arranged them in a narrative order, consider how the photo record would be different if someone else took the images of your life. For example, what choices might your mother make if she held the camera? How would her record of your day differ from yours? Use the PREWRITING QUESTIONS below to begin your analysis of the photographs you have taken of your life, work, and leisure.

PREWRITING QUESTIONS

- **Mediation.** How is the presence of the creator felt in these images, even if the person who has taken the photographs is absent from the scene?

- **Representation.** Who is included in the images? What is the ethnicity of the subjects? What is their social class? What is their gender? What are their ages? Are any of the settings, poses, or activities stereotypical for the groups who are represented in the frame?

- **Absence.** Is there anything that these images are not telling us? What is outside the frame, perhaps known only to the person who took the photographs?

- **Story.** Do the images represent a special story? Is the story so universal and apparent that anyone could make up a story to accompany these pictures?

- **Props.** What does the clothing of the subjects say about the era that the photographs were taken? Does clothing reveal anything significant about social class? Are the human subjects in the photographs performing stereotypical roles for men and women? Are they holding any props (trophies, sports equipment, instruments) that indicate something about their interests?

On Display: Working

Some famous photographs have been taken of the American working class in the last century. Your project for this ON DISPLAY assignment is to write a story about either of the images of workers displayed below on page 112. Who will be your main character? Will the photographer narrate the story? Or will you select one of the subjects? If your classmates have written their narratives from a different point of view, compare the way that the point of view changes the story that is told.

Jacob A. Riis (1849–1914) lived and worked in New York City in the late nineteenth century. His exposé *How the Other Half Lives* (1890) and includes engravings made from his photographs. (One of his photographs appears in Chapter One.) Riis states in the preface to his book that he was inspired by the "belief that every man's experience ought to be worth something to the community," no matter how impoverished the conditions in which that man lived. The title was inspired by the saying that "one half of the world does not know how the other half lives," that those who have wealth and leisure do not know or care about the struggles of the underclass. Lewis Hine (1874–1940) used his documentary photographs to generate legislation barring child labor in the United States. Between 1908 and 1918, Hine, employed by the National Child Labor Committee, traveled to factories, fields, and mines to photograph and interview children at work. These photographs were reproduced in newspapers and in publications of the National Child Labor Committee, and displayed during public lectures.

In 2003, Bread and Roses, a not-for-profit arts group in New York City, attempted a similar documentary project to those of Riis and Hine. Rather than sending an established photojournalist into the field, though, the group provided area workers with point-and-click cameras and gave them training in photography so that they might document the aspects of their lives that were most important to them. Many of these immigrant workers had not previously had a camera. Having a camera was "a dream come true," in the words of one of the participants in the Unseen America project. "When I work hard I want to remember it," Ping Lam, a garment worker, told Anthony De Palma from the *New York Times*. Many of the images created by the amateur photographers depict people at work. Many are also positive images, stressing the workers' need to make their work visible to a wider audience.

- Identify some of the everyday objects that represent the workers in the images. How are these everyday material artifacts indicative of human lives and lived experiences?

- Ling's photograph is accompanied by an explanatory text, reproduced here. Her attitude toward the herb store is favorable and reinforces Riis's idea that "every man's experience ought to be worth something to the community." Would your interpretation of the image change if you were not aware of the text?

- How does the meaning of Ling's photograph change when it is paired with this image by Lewis Hine of children in factories?

Chinese Herb Store, *Tang Chi Ling*

unseenamerica, an ongoing project of
1199SEIU's Bread and Roses Cultural Project

Chinese herbs have been used to cure diseases, save people, and keep us healthy for thousands of years. These plants can do many things. All of the little drawers on the wall are filled with Chinese herbs.

Barefoot Boy Works on Factory Machinery, Georgia.

Photo: © Bettman/Corbis.

Glossary

Absences. A term advanced by theorists working with the school of philosophy and literary analysis called deconstruction, absences are elements or ideas within a text or a visual medium that are left out, either consciously or unconsciously. The reader must examine such gaps, searching for what is not represented in order to fully grasp the artist's intention.

Abstract. Disassociated from a particular object, abstract information is reduced to elemental components, such as geometry, line, and color. Abstract art is removed from a one-to-one correspondence with physical objects, the human figure, or landscape so that there is little or no realistic or representational content in the image.

Affect. A psychoanalytic approach to emotions, affect theory examines humans' sources of emotions and responses in connection to images.

Angle. The position or direction from which an image is viewed. Spectators may look on the scene or object from above, below, outside, or inside.

Applied criticism. An interpretation that one writer (usually an art critic, historian, or teacher) has created about an image, using biographical, historical, or theoretical works.

Arrangement. The specific order and placement of the individual elements of an image. Also see **principles of design**.

Asymmetrical. Lacking in harmony and spatial balance. The image may contain different elements on each side.

Backstory. Another word for background information, the *backstory* refers to circumstances that occur prior to the beginning of a narrative. In the study of images, it refers to the surrounding information about people and events that surround the slice of life represented in the still photo or painting.

Balance. The harmonious position of objects within an image, frequently brought about because of the symmetrical arrangement of similar or complementary elements.

Cartoon. A one-dimensional drawing, often satiric, unrealistic, or political, that purposefully combines text and images to affect the viewer.

Color. The eye perceives color as various wavelengths of light reflected by different surfaces. Colors are identified by name, hue, tint, or intensity. Color schemes include primary colors (red, yellow, blue), secondary colors (orange, green, violet), and tertiary (the uneven mixture of primary colors). Color schemes can be warm (reds and oranges) or cool (blues).

Composition. The arrangement of an image's various **formal elements**, such as color, shape, and contrast.

Contrast. The difference in visual properties that makes an object stand out from other objects in an image. Combining objects of varying colors, degrees of light, or age effectively creates contrast.

Convention. An accepted, established artistic practice or technique. *Convention* also refers to the repetition of accepted styles or modes of interpretation and can mean that a way of seeing has become habitual.

Critique. The product of a critic's judgment and evaluation of an image from his or her personal point of view.

Cultural context. The societal framework unique to a specific people group, including morals, values, and traditions, which acts as a lens through which ideas are viewed and interpreted.

Deconstruction. The theory of analyzing **absences** in images. As a critical theory, deconstruction originates from the work of French philosopher Jacques Derrida. Deconstruction urges viewers to "read against the grain," looking for **latent content** within an image.

Discrimination. The act of making fine distinctions between different elements that compose an image's whole.

Dividing line. An implied or inscribed line indicating the center-point of an image.

Dominance. Specific emphasis that highlights certain elements within an image over others. Weight, line, shape, texture, and color all bring objects to the fore as dominant components of an image.

Elements of design. These components dictate an image's literal appearance through seven aspects: color, value, line, shape, form, texture, and space.

Formal criticism. The study of specific **elements of design** pertaining to a work of art. Formal critics are more concerned with aspects of form (see **Formal elements**) than the content or meaning of a particular image.

Formal elements. Distinguishing, essential conventions, also called visual elements, which artists manipulate to create works of art. Formal elements include, but are not limited to, point, line, color, texture, and shape.

Gaze. The process of focused, prolonged looking that engages personal emotion, memory, and ideology in forming judgments.

Genre. A specific, highly specialized category of art marked by form, content, or style. While identifying genre may be a useful step in classifying a work, such a process may not account for all aspects of that work. Many artists incorporate elements from several genres to produce an effective image.

Grid. A framework of intersecting horizontal and vertical lines that cross the surface of an image to form sections. A center point (or dividing line) may create mirrored halves that pattern the image.

Heritage tourism. The desire to experience the past through **living history** displays, costumed reenactment, and the restoration of both buildings and landscapes to their original, pre-consumer, pre-modern appearance.

Historic integrity. The restorative effort to return historically significant land to its original appearance through such actions as burying utility lines and returning buildings to their original condition and interior design.

History paintings. Artwork portraying religious, historical, literary, or mythological subjects that embody an interpretation of life or project a moral or didactic message.

Horizon line. The invisible horizontal line that marks the division between earth and sky.

Iconography. From *eikon*, meaning symbol, and *graph*, meaning writing, iconography is the use of symbols to represent ideas. Native American cave paintings are one example of iconography.

Ideology. The values, concepts, and philosophies unique to an individual, a society, or a culture. These beliefs guide our perceptions and actions, defining what is permissible and what is abnormal within our social group.

Illuminators. A term given to book illustrators working in the European Middle Ages, who utilized a complex visual language of symbols, called **iconography**.

Illustrations. Visual representations of something in a text that highlight a specific concept or idea.

Intertextuality. The relationship between two or more images, one imitating another, that connect through shared quotations, images, or allusions and cause viewers to rethink the meaning of the original image as well as its imitation. Some theorists believe that all images are interdependent; that is, texts continually refer to each other in a relationship of intertextuality.

Latent content.   A product of Freudian psychoanalysis, latent content focuses on the elements of an artist's unconscious that are reflected in his or her works. Latent content is the opposite of **manifest content**, which is the part of a work that reveals the artist's conscious mind.

Limners.   Untrained and generally anonymous artists who specialized in portrait painting in the early American colonies.

Literal elements.   Readily observable components of an image, such as gradients of color and shadow. See **elements of design** and **principles of design**.

Living history.   Displays in which modern-day people assume the costume, language, and daily tasks and activities, such as spinning and farming, of people who lived in a certain historical period. Visitors to living history displays can observe the past as if it were still present.

Manifest content.   All texts contain elements that are immediately evident and show us what the creators wanted us to see. Conversely, **latent content** exists within absences, revealing the prejudices of the creators or demonstrating unconscious misgivings about the subjects.

Mediate.   When speaking of the interpretation of literary and visual media, it is currently assumed that all information is mentally filtered by an ideological screen, that no information is received without first being affected and shaped by the values, concepts, and philosophies held by individuals and societies.

Multimodality.   The capacity to simultaneously communicate with sound, image, and tactile sensation. This term was pioneered by Günther Kress; see his works for more information on the linguistic analysis of multimodality.

Mythology.   Interconnected tales that account for significant historical miraculous or religious occurrences within a culture. Individual stories, called myths, are related to social traditions. A culture's mythology is similar to its legends, which focus on the feats of specific heroes or heroines, and from parables or fables, which serve a moral or didactic purpose.

Narratives.   Presentations or representations of stories in visual or verbal form.

Orthogonal.   Composed of right angles. When perceived vertical lines come together on the **vanishing point** of the **horizon line**, these converging lines are called orthogonal lines.

Pattern.   The repetition of elements in an image. Patterns may be abstract, linear (as in plaid), or representational.

Picturesque.   Possessing a quality of scenic, natural beauty. **Conventions** of the picturesque developed in eighteenth century Europe persist today. They dictated that scenes and views be divided into pleasing, regular **planes** of foreground, middleground, and background. In America, rugged mountains and vast prairies became as awe inspiring as the majestic architecture of Europe, and viewers became entranced by a new manifestation of the picturesque.

Plane.   A flat surface or an area within the field of vision. Planes may be divided into foreground, middleground, and background.

Point of view.   The relationship of the viewer to the image. As in **vantage point**, the point of view of an image is created by the painter or photographer and refers to the implied position of a viewer.

Principles of design.   Arrangement of individual elements of an image into a form that provides meaning.

Propaganda.   A specific type of visual or verbal message designed to promote a particular agenda. Often evoking an emotional response from the viewer, images of propaganda purposely work to influence the viewer's decisions. Propaganda is used frequently in political campaigns and during wartime.

Proportion.   The compatible relationship between objects of the same size and weight. The size and quantity of the elements is measured according to standards of perspective and customs of representing the real.

Radial.   Elements of an image are organized by using a circle as a design template.

Recursive.   Characterized by an ability to occur again. In analytical practice, returning to look again and write again about an image or object invokes a recursive process.

Representation; representational.   Visual information is processed on the level of objects found in the environment. We sometimes refer to representation as "realism."

Scholarship.   Scholars work from documents to position an image in its cultural, historical, and biographical milieu.

Symbol; symbolic representation.   This level of visual information takes the form of conventional systems of communication in which humans have constructed signs and attached meaning to them. Symbols must be simple in order to be immediately remembered, recognized, and replicated.

Symmetrical.   Having corresponding size and shape within a particular plane; balanced.

Theoretical criticism.   Theoretical criticism works with an identifiable, defined school of interpretation, an idea from a prominent theorist, or a critical term. **Deconstruction** is an example of one such critical approach.

Three-dimensional.   Involving three dimensions or aspects, giving the impression of depth to an image.

Transparency.   The concept of an image as a lens or a window to reality.

Transtextuality.   A term introduced by French narrative theorist Gerard Genette to describe everything—whether **latent** or **manifest**— that places a text in a relationship with other texts. Genette views **intertextuality** as just one form of interconnectedness between texts. For additional information, see Genette's *Palimpsests: Literature in the Second Degree* (1997).

Two-dimensional.   Involving only two dimensions or aspects (usually length and width), giving the impression of flatness or lack of depth to an image.

Value.   A term specific to the **elements of design,** value refers to the graduated scale of whiteness of an image. White is at one end of the scale of color values; black is at the other.

Vanishing point.   The point within an image where parallel lines seem to converge.

Vantage point.   The spectators' position relative to the image being viewed.

Vernacular landscape.   A timeless, everyday style of land use and development based on needs and habits. According to John Brinckerhoff Jackson, who adapts the term vernacular landscape in *Discovering the Vernacular Landscape* (1984), landscape itself is man-made, not natural. Humans build to suit particular needs and wants. **Vernacular architecture** is concerned with ordinary domestic and commercial buildings rather than those that are picturesque or monumental.

Visual culture.   The surrounding image-based aspects of our society, including fashion, architecture, film, and advertisements.

Visual literacy.   The ability to read and analyze visual culture, just as we are able to read and analyze print media such as novels and newspapers.

Visual purity.   Restored time-period accuracy given to sites of historical significance, so that present-day visitors can experience the same visual experiences as the previous generations.

Visual rhetoric. Understanding the persuasive properties of images and visual cultural elements.

Weight (Using line, shape, and texture). The degree of **dominance** of an image's various elements as they contrast through varying elements, such as line, shape, and texture.

Bibliography

Chapter One

Arnheim, Rudolf. *Toward a Psychology of Art: Collected Essays.* Berkeley: U of California P, 1966.

—. *Visual Thinking.* Berkeley: U of California P, 1969.

Barnard, Malcolm. *Approaches to Understanding Visual Culture.* New York: Palgrave, 2001.

Barrie, J. M. *Peter Pan.* New York: Charles Scribner's Sons, 1906.

Benstock, Shari, and Suzanne Ferris. *Footnotes: On Shoes.* New Brunswick, NJ: Rutgers UP, 2001.

Bryson, Norman, ed. *Visual Culture: Images and Interpretations.* Hanover: UP of New England [for] Wesleyan UP, 1994.

Carson, Fiona, and Claire Pajaczkowska, eds. *Feminist Visual Culture.* New York: Routledge, 2001.

Cronon, William. "Telling Tales on Canvas: Landscapes of Frontier Change." *Discovered Lands, Invented Pasts: Transforming Visions of the American West.* Ed. Jules David Prown. New Haven: Yale UP, 1992.

Doy, Gen. *Black Visual Culture: Modernity and Postmodernity.* New York: I. B. Tauris, 2000.

Evans, Jessica, and Stuart Hall, eds. *Visual Culture: The Reader.* Thousand Oaks, CA: Sage, 1999.

Heywood, Ian, and Barry Sandywell, eds. *Interpreting Visual Culture: Explorations in the Hermeneutics of the Visual.* New York: Routledge, 1999.

Hovanec, Carol P. and David Freund. "Photographs, Writing, and Critical Thinking." *Images in Langauge, Media, and Mind.* Ed. Roy F. Fox. Urbana, Illinois: NCTE, 1994. 42–57.

Jenks, Chris, ed. *Visual Culture.* New York: Routledge, 1995.

Jowett, Garth S., and Victoria O'Donnell, *Propaganda and Persuasion.* 3rd ed. Thousand Oaks, CA: Sage, 1999.

Marlin, Randal. *Propaganda and the Ethics of Persuasion.* Orchard Park, NY: Broadview Press, 2002.

McCloud, Scott. *Understanding Comics.* Northampton, MA: Kitchen Sink Press, 1993.

McLuhan, Marshall. *The Mechanical Bride: Folklore of Industrial Man.* New York: Vanguard P, 1951.

Messaris, Paul. *Visual "Literacy": Image, Mind, and Reality.* Boulder: Westview P, 1994.

Mirzoeff, Nicholas. *An Introduction to Visual Culture.* New York: Routledge, 1999.

Poltarnees, Welleran. *All Mirrors Are Magic Mirrors: Reflections on Pictures Found in Children's Books.* La Jolla, CA: Green Tiger Press, 1972.

Robertson, George. *The Block Reader in Visual Culture.* New York: Routledge, 1996.

Scholes, Robert. *Protocols of Reading.* New Haven: Yale UP, 1989.

Silbermann, Alphons, and H. D. Dryoff, eds. *Comics and Visual Culture: Research Studies from Ten Countries.* New York: K. G. Saur, 1986.

Sturken, Marita. *Practices of Looking: An Introduction of Visual Culture.* New York: Oxford UP, 2001.

Visual Learning Center. Polaroid. **www.polaroid.com/work/teachers/vlc/index.jsp.**

Walker, John A., and Sarah Chaplin. *Visual Culture: An Introduction.* Manchester, UK: Manchester UP, 1997.

Chapter Two

Artlex Art Dictionary. **www.artlex.com.**

Barnett, Sylvan. *A Short Guide to Writing About Art.* 4th ed. New York: Harper Collins, 1993.

Burns, Robert. "My Love Is Like a Red, Red Rose." *The Essential Burns.* Ed. Robert Creeley. New York: Ecco Press, 1989.

Derrida, Jacques. *Writing and Difference.* Trans. Alan Bass. Chicago: U of Chicago P, 1978.

Dondis, Donis A. *A Primer of Visual Literacy.* Cambridge, MA: MIT P, 1973.

Eliot, George. *Middlemarch.* New York: Modern Library, 1994.

Fraser, Antonia. *A Splash of Red.* New York: Norton, 1982.

Jauss, Hans Robert. *Toward an Aesthetic of Reception.* Trans. Timothy Bahti. Minneapolis: U of Minnesota P, 1982.

Mulvey, Laura. "Visual Pleasure and Narrative Cinema." *Visual and Other Pleasures.* London: Macmillan, 1989.

Platzner, Rebecca and Kay E. Vandergrift. "Notes on Creating a Visual Interpretive Analysis." 20 January 2002. **http://www.scils.rutgers.edu/~kvander/Syllabus/creation.html.**

Sassoon, Rosemary, and Albertine Gaur. *Signs, Symbols, and Icons: Pre-History to the Computer Age.* Exeter, UK: Intellect, 1997.

Vandergrift Kay, and Rebecca Platzner. *Notes on Creating a Visual Interpretive Analysis.* **http://www.scils.rutgers.edu/~kvander/Syllabus/creation.html.**
Zelizer, Barbie. *Remembering to Forget: The Holocaust Through the Camera's Eye.* Chicago: U of Chicago P, 1998.

Websites of Interest

Artchive. **http://artchive.com/.**
Branton, Bev. *Visual Literacy.* **Vicu.utoronto.ca/staff/branton/homep.htm.**
Burkhardt, Robert, *Visual Literacy Exercises.* **www.chanel1com/users/bobwb/vlit/index.htm.**
Learning to Look: A Format for Looking at and Talking About Photographs. Center for Creative Photography. **http://www.library.arizona.edu/branches/ccp/education/guides/reframe/lookguid.htm.**
March, Tom. *ArtSpeak 101.* **http://www.kn.pacbell.com/wired/art2/artspeak/home.html.**

Structuralism

Culler, Jonathan. *Structuralist Poetics: Structuralism, Linguistics and the Study of Literature.* New York: Routledge, 2002.
Saussure, Ferdinand de. *Course in General Linguistics.* Ed. Charles Bally and Albert Sechehaye. Trans. Roy Harris. LaSalle, IL: Open Court, 1986.

Deconstruction

Derrida, Jacques. *Negotiations: Interventions and Interviews, 1971–2001.* Trans. Elizabeth Rottenberg. Stanford, CA: Stanford UP, 2002.
Kamuf, Peggy, ed. *A Derrida Reader: Between the Blinds.* New York: Columbia UP, 1991.
Wolfreys, Julian, ed. *A Derrida Reader: Writing Performances.* Edinburgh: Edinburgh UP, 1998.

Feminism, Gender, and Queer Theories

Butler, Judith. *Gender Trouble: Feminism and the Subversion of Identity.* New York: Routledge, 1999.
Eagleton, Mary, ed. *Feminist Literary Criticism.* New York: Longman, 1991.
Sedgwick, Eva Kosofsky. *Epistemology of the Closet.* Berkeley: U of California P, 1990.

Psychoanalytic

Badcock, Christopher, ed. *Essential Freud.* 2nd ed. Cambridge, MA: Blackwell, 1992.

Benvenuto, Bice, and Roger Kennedy. *The Works of Jacques Lacan: An Introduction.* New York: St. Martin's P, 1986.

Gay, Peter, ed. *The Freud Reader.* New York: Norton, 1989.

Lacan, Jacques. *Écrits: A Selection.* Trans. Alan Sheridan. New York: Norton, 1977.

Cultural Studies, New Historicism, and Cultural Poetics

Gates, Henry Louis, Jr., ed. *"Race," Writing, and Difference.* Chicago: U of Chicago P, 1986.

Hall, Stuart, ed. *Culture, Media, Language: Working Papers in Cultural Studies, 1972–79.* Birmingham, UK: Centre for Contemporary Cultural Studies, U of Birmingham, 1980.

Williams, Raymond. *Culture and Society, 1780–1950.* New York: Columbia UP, 1983.

Marxism

Althusser, Louis. *Essays on Ideology.* London: Verso, 1984.

Benjamin, Walter. "The Work of Art of the Age of Mechanical Reproduction." *Illuminations.* Ed. Hannah Arendt. Trans. Harry Zohn. New York: Schocken, 1968.

Gramsci, Antonio. *The Gramsci Reader: Selected Writings, 1916–1935.* Ed. David Forgasc. New York: New York UP, 2000.

Jameson, Fredric. *Postmodernism, or The Cultural Logic of Late Capitalism.* Durham, NC: Duke UP, 1991.

Chapter Three

Baudrillard, Jean. *Simulacra and Simulation.* Trans. Sheila Faria Glaser. Ann Arbor: U of Michigan P, 1994.

Bennett, Tony. *The Birth of the Museum: History, Theory, Politics.* New York: Routledge, 1995.

Bird, Isabella. *A Lady's Life in the Rocky Mountains.* 1879. Norman: U of Oklahoma P, 1960.

Blair, Carole. "Commemorating in the Theme Park Zone: Reading the Astronauts Memorial." *At the Intersection: Cultural Studies and Rhetorical Studies.* Ed. Thomas Rosteck. New York: Guilford P, 1999. 29–73.

Burgin, Victor. *In/Different Spaces: Place and Memory in Visual Culture.* Berkeley: U of California P, 1996.

Dickinson, Greg. "Joe's Rhetoric: Starbucks and the Spatial Rhetoric of Authenticity." *Rhetoric Society Quarterly.* 32(2002): 5–28.

Doane, Gustavus C. "Official Report of the Washburn-Langford-Doane Expedition into the Upper Yellowstone in 1870." Washington, D. C.: National Archives. Original MS, Dec. 15, 1870.

Haines, Aubrey L. *Yellowstone National Park: Its Exploration and Establishment.* Washington, DC: U.S. Department of the Interior National Park Service, 1974. **http://www.cr.nps.gov/history/online_books/haines1/index.htm.**

Hooper-Greenhill, Eilean. *Museums and the Interpretation of Visual Culture.* New York: Routledge, 2000.

Jackson, John Brinckerhoff. *Discovering the Vernacular Landscape.* New Haven: Yale UP, 1984.

Kress, Gunther, and Theo van Leeuwen. *Multimodal Discourse: The Modes and Media of Contemporary Communication.* London: Arnold, 2001.

Lincoln, Abraham. Gettysburg Address. 19 Nov. 1863. Library of Congress, 14 Apr. 2003. **http://www.loc.gov/exhibits/gadd/4403.html.**

Linenthal, Edward Tabor. *Sacred Ground: Americans and Their Battlefields.* 2nd ed. Urbana: U of Illinois P, 1993.

Lubbren, Nina, and David Crouch, eds. *Visual Culture and Tourism.* New York: Berg, 2003.

Marling, Karal Ann. *Designing Disney's Theme Parks: The Architecture of Reassurance.* New York: Flammarion, 1997.

Mattes, Merrill. *Colter's Hell and Jackson's Hole: The Fur Trappers' Exploration of the Yellowstone and Grand Teton Park Region.* Yellowstone Library and Museum Association, 1962. **http://www.cr.nps.gov/history/online_books/grte1/**

Moran, Thomas Letter to F. V. Hayden. 11 March 1872. Washington, D.C.: National Archives. (M623, roll 2, frames 468–70).

Osborne, Peter. *Traveling Light: Photography, Travel, and Visual Culture.* New York: Manchester UP, 2000.

Rogoff, Irit. *Terra Infirma: Geography's Visual Culture.* New York: Routledge, 2000.

Stern, Robert A. M. *Pride of Place: Building the American Dream.* New York: American Heritage, 1986.

Weeks, Jim. *Gettysburg: Memory, Market, and an American Shrine.* Princeton, NJ: Princeton UP, 2003.

Websites of Interest

Colonial Williamsburg. **http://www.history.org/.**
Harper's Ferry (NPS). **www.nps.gov/hafe/home.htm.**
Jorvik Viking Centre. **www.jorvik-viking-centre.co.uk/.**
Mystic Seaport. **www.mysticseaport.org.**
National Register of Historic Places. **http://www.cr.nps.gov/nr/.**
Old Sturbridge Village. **http://www.osv.org/.**
Plimoth Plantation. **www.plimoth.org.**

Chapter Four

"Abraham Zapruder Interview." The Sixth Floor Museum and Dealey Plaza. **http://www.jfk.org/Reasearch/Zapruder/Transcript.htm.**

Belting, Hans. *Likeness and Presence: A History of the Image Before the Era of Art.* Trans. Edmund Jephcott. Chicago: U of Chicago P, 1994.

Bloom, Lisa, ed. *With Other Eyes: Looking at Race and Gender in Visual Culture.* Minneapolis: U of Minnesota P, 1999.

Carroll, Lewis. *Alice's Adventures in Wonderland.* Illus. John Tenniel. Philadelphia: Lippincott, 1923.

DePalma, Anthony. "Caméra Vérité; A Peek Through Blue Collar Lenses." *New York Times* 18 June 2003: B1.

Frye, Judith. *Women's Camera Work: Self/Body/Other in American Visual Culture.* Durham, NC: Duke UP, 1998.

Geertz, Clifford. "Being There." *Works and Lives: The Anthropologist as Author.* Stanford, CA: Stanford UP, 1988.

"'GBP 5,000 payoff' for Tourist Whose Photos Were Lost." *Daily Mail* (London). 9 June 2003. 19.

Hirsch, Marianne. *Family Frames: Photography, Narrative, and Postmemory.* Cambridge, MA: Harvard UP, 1997.

Hünig, Wolfgand K. *British and German Cartoons as Weapons in World War I: Invectives and Ideology of Political Cartoons, a Cognitive Linguistics Approach.* New York: Lang, 2002.

Kuhn, Annette. *Family Secrets: Acts of Memory and Imagination.* New York: Verso, 1995.

Lippard, Lucy R. *On the Beaten Track: Tourism, Art, and Place.* New York: New Press, 1999.

Minear, Richard H. *Dr. Seuss Goes to War: The World War II Editorial Cartoons of Theodor Seuss Geisel.* New York: New Press, 2001.

Morris, Susan. *A Teacher's Guide to Using Portraits.* Swindon, UK: English Heritage, 1989.

Obra, Joan. "Specialty Camera Stores Scramble to Adapt to Growth of Digital Photography." *The Fresno Bee.* 18 Nov. 2003.

Osborne, Peter. *Traveling Light: Photography, Travel and Visual Culture.* Manchester, UK; New York: Manchester UP, 2000.

PMA Marketing Research. Photo Marketing Association. **http://www.pmai.org/**.

Riis, Jacob. *How the Other Half Lives: Studies Among the Tenements of New York.* New York: Scribner's, 1890.

Theroux, Paul. "The Cerebral Snapshot." *Sunrise with Seamonsters.* New York: Houghton Mifflin, 1985.

Websites of Interest

Library of Congress American Memory. **www.loc.gov.**

Index

127